Sally J. Kenney
Helen Kinsella
Editors

Politics and Feminist Standpoint Theories

Politics and Feminist Standpoint Theories has been co-published simultaneously as *Women & Politics*, Volume 18, Number 3 1997.

Pre-publication
REVIEWS,
COMMENTARIES,
EVALUATIONS . . .

"**T**HIS ILLUMINATING COLLECTION OF ESSAYS reveals the importance of standpoint theory as an essentially contested notion–as a site, a cleared space, enabling reflection and dialogue on human experience, identity, objectivity, rationality, scientific method, and the politics of knowledge. . . . This collection will be useful to scholars and students interested in exploring how we should understand the explosion in knowledge generated by feminist projects."

Sandra Harding, PhD
Professor
Education and Women's Studies
UCLA

Politics and Feminist Standpoint Theories

Politics and Feminist Standpoint Theories has been co-published simultaneously as *Women & Politics*, Volume 18, Number 3 1997.

Politics and Feminist Standpoint Theories

Sally J. Kenney
Helen Kinsella
Editors

Politics and Feminist Standpoint Theories has been co-published simultaneously as *Women & Politics*, Volume 18, Number 3 1997.

The Haworth Press, Inc.
New York • London

Politics and Feminist Standpoint Theories has been co-published simultaneously as *Women & Politics*, Volume 18, Number 3 1997.

The Haworth Press, Inc., 10 Alice Street, Binghamton, NY 13904-1580 USA

Cover design by Thomas J. Mayshock Jr.

Library of Congress Cataloging-in-Publication Data

Politics and feminist standpoint theories / Sally J. Kenney, Helen Kinsella, editors.
     p. cm.
     "Has also been published as Women & politics, volume 18, number 3, 1997"–T.p. verso.
     Includes bibliographical references and index.
     ISBN 0-7890-0364-3 (alk. paper).–ISBN 0-7890-0366-X (alk. paper)
     1. Feminist theory. 2. Hartsock, Nancy C. M. Money, sex, and power. 3. Women's studies. I. Kenney, Sally Jane. II. Kinsella, Helen.
HQ1190.P65 1997
305.42′01–dc21
                                                        97-37008
                                                         CIP

INDEXING & ABSTRACTING

Contributions to this publication are selectively indexed or abstracted in print, electronic, online, or CD-ROM version(s) of the reference tools and information services listed below. This list is current as of the copyright date of this publication. See the end of this section for additional notes.

- *ABC POL SCI: A Bibliography of Contents: Political Science & Government*, ABC-CLIO, Inc., 130 Cremona Drive, Santa Barbara, CA 93117

- *Academic Abstracts/CD-ROM*, EBSCO Publishing Editorial Department, P.O. Box 590, Ipswich, MA 01938-0590

- *Academic Index (on-line)*, Information Access Company, 362 Lakeside Drive, Foster City, CA 94404

- *Academic Search: data base of 2,000 selected academic serials, updated monthly*, EBSCO Publishing, 83 Pine Street, Peabody, MA 01960

- *America: History and Life*, ABC-CLIO, Inc., 130 Cremona Drive, Santa Barbara, CA 93117

- *CNPIEC Reference Guide: Chinese National Directory of Foreign Periodicals*, P.O. Box 88, Beijing, People's Republic of China

- *Current Contents .... see: Institute for Scientific Information*

- *Current Legal Sociology*, International Institute for the Sociology of Law, Ap. 28, 20560 ONATI, GIPUZKOA, Spain

- *Expanded Academic Index*, Information Access Company, 362 Lakeside Drive, Forest City, CA 94404

- *Feminist Periodicals: A Current Listing of Contents*, Women's Studies Librarian-at-Large, 728 State Street, 430 Memorial Library, Madison, WI 53706

(continued)

- *Historical Abstracts*, ABC-CLIO Library, 130 Cremona Drive, Santa Barbara, CA 93117

- *IBZ International Bibliography of Periodical Literature*, Zeller Verlag GmbH & Co., P.O.B. 1949, D-49009 Osnabruck, Germany

- *Index to Periodical Articles Related to Law*, University of Texas, 727 East 26th Street, Austin, TX 78705

- *Institute for Scientific Information*, 3501 Market Street, Philadelphia, PA 19104-3302 (USA). Coverage in:
  a) Social Science Citation Index (SSCI): print, online, CD-ROM
  b) Research Alert (current awareness service)
  c) Social SciSearch (magnetic tape)
  d) Current Contents/Social & Behavioral Sciences (weekly current awareness service)

- *International Political Science Abstracts*, 27 Rue Saint-Guillaume, F-75337 Paris, Cedex 07, France

- *INTERNET ACCESS (& additional networks) Bulletin Board for Libraries ("BUBL") coverage of information resources on INTERNET, JANET, and other networks.*
  - <URL:http://bubl.ac.uk/>
  - The new locations will be found under <URL:http://bubl.ac.uk/link/>.
  - Any existing BUBL users who have problems finding information on the new service should contact the BUBL help line by sending e-mail to <bubl@bubl.ac.uk>.
  The Andersonian Library, Curran Building, 101 St. James Road, Glasgow G4 0NS, Scotland

- *MasterFILE: updated database from EBSCO Publishing*, EBSCO Publishing, 83 Pine Street, Peabody, MA 01960

- *Periodica Islamica*, Berita Publishing, 22 Jalan Liku, 59100 Kuala Lumpur, Malaysia

(continued)

- *Periodical Abstracts, Research I (general & basic reference indexing & abstracting data-base from University Microfilms International (UMI), 300 North Zeeb Road, P.O. Box 1346, Ann Arbor, MI 48106-1346)*, UMI Data Courier, P.O. Box 32770, Louisville, KY 40232-2770

- *Periodical Abstracts, Research II (broad coverage indexing & abstracting data-base from University Microfilms International (UMI), 300 North Zeeb Road, P.O. Box 1346, Ann Arbor, MI 48106-1346)*, UMI Data Courier, P.O. Box 32770, Louisville, KY 40232-2770

- *Political Science Abstracts*, IFI/Plenum Data Company, 3202 Kirkwood Highway, Wilmington, DE 19808

- *Public Affairs Information Bulletin (PAIS)*, Public Affairs Information Service, Inc., 521 West 43rd Street, New York, NY 10036-4396

- *Social Planning/Policy & Development Abstracts (SOPODA)*, Sociological Abstracts, Inc., P.O. Box 22206, San Diego, CA 92192-0206

- *Social Science Citation Index . . . . see: Institute for Scientific Information*

- *Social Work Abstracts*, National Association of Social Workers, 750 First Street NW, 8th Floor, Washington, DC 20002

- *Sociological Abstracts (SA)*, Sociological Abstracts, Inc., P.O. Box 22206, San Diego, CA 92192-0206

- *Studies on Women Abstracts*, Carfax Publishing Company, P.O. Box 25, Abingdon, Oxfordshire OX14 3UE, United Kingdom

- *Women Studies Abstracts*, Rush Publishing Company, P.O. Box 1, Rush, NY 14543

- *Women's Studies Index (indexed comprehensively)*, G.K. Hall & Co., 1633 Broadway, 5th Floor, New York, NY 10019

(continued)

SPECIAL BIBLIOGRAPHIC NOTES

related to special journal issues (separates)
and indexing/abstracting

☐ indexing/abstracting services in this list will also cover material in any "separate" that is co-published simultaneously with Haworth's special thematic journal issue or DocuSerial. Indexing/abstracting usually covers material at the article/chapter level.

☐ monographic co-editions are intended for either non-subscribers or libraries which intend to purchase a second copy for their circulating collections.

☐ monographic co-editions are reported to all jobbers/wholesalers/approval plans. The source journal is listed as the "series" to assist the prevention of duplicate purchasing in the same manner utilized for books-in-series.

☐ to facilitate user/access services all indexing/abstracting services are encouraged to utilize the co-indexing entry note indicated at the bottom of the first page of each article/chapter/contribution.

☐ this is intended to assist a library user of any reference tool (whether print, electronic, online, or CD-ROM) to locate the monographic version if the library has purchased this version but not a subscription to the source journal.

☐ individual articles/chapters in any Haworth publication are also available through the Haworth Document Delivery Service (HDDS).

Politics and Feminist Standpoint Theories

CONTENTS

ABOUT THE EDITORS

Sally J. Kenney, PhD, has been an Associate Professor at the Humphrey Institute of Public Affairs and the Director of the Center on Women and Public Policy at the University of Minnesota in Minneapolis since 1995. Prior to coming to Minnesota, Kenney held joint appointments in political science and women's studies at the University of Iowa. She is the author of *For Whose Protection? Reproductive Hazards and Exclusionary Policies in the United States and Britain* (University of Michigan Press). Her research and writing interests include exclusionary employment policies, comparative law and politics, gender and political institutions, feminist organizations, the European Court of Justice, and social policy in the European Community.

Helen Kinsella, MA, is a PhD candidate in political science at the University of Minnesota. She has an MA in public affairs from the Humphrey Institute and a graduate minor in feminist studies. Her research focuses on international networks on violence against women, Latin American politics, and feminist political theory.

Introduction

Sally J. Kenney

In 1994, Nancy Hirschmann organized a panel entitled "The Feminist Standpoint Ten Years Later: Roundtable on Nancy Hartsock's *Money, Sex, and Power*" for the annual meeting of the American Political Science Association. Nancy Hartsock, Susan Hekman, Sara Ruddick, Peregrine Schwartz-Shea, and Sandra Harding each gave papers. I was drawn to the panel by pedagogical concerns. During the seven years I taught the introductory feminist theory course for Women's Studies at the University of Iowa, I never felt that I managed to successfully convey the gist of feminist standpoint theory. In the class, we read Patricia Hill Collins, Nancy Hartsock, Sandra Harding, and others in different orders and in different combinations. Part of the difficulty was that many students lacked a basic vocabulary and facility with philosophical concepts. They were interested in feminism but knew little about materialism, liberalism, psychoanalysis, postmodernism, or, most importantly, epistemology. I assigned Harding's article on "The Instability of Analytical Categories" (1986) but, while I had found it enormously helpful in clarifying standpoint theories, the students were as confused or misinformed as ever. Nancy Hartsock, Sandra Harding, Patricia Hill Collins, and Dorothy Smith's commentary on Susan Hekman's article in *Signs* (22:2 [1997]) claiming their work has been misunderstood and misconstrued suggests that confusion and disagreement about interpretation and meaning is not confined to novices.

Harding's project of categorizing schools of feminist thought is a tricky business for the teacher, scholar, or student alike. We can trace the evolving taxonomies of feminist theory either through introductory feminist theory (or women's studies) texts or in the changing array of canonical

[Haworth co-indexing entry note]: "Introduction." Kenney, Sally J. Co-published simultaneously in *Women & Politics* (The Haworth Press, Inc.) Vol. 18, No. 3, 1997, pp. 1-5; and: *Politics and Feminist Standpoint Theories* (ed: Sally J. Kenney and Helen Kinsella) The Haworth Press, Inc., 1997, pp. 1-5. Single or multiple copies of this article are available for a fee from The Haworth Document Delivery Service [1-800-342-9678, 9:00 a.m. - 5:00 p.m. (EST). E-mail address: getinfo@haworth.com].

1

theorists feminist scholars survey and cite at the outset of their writings. The "brands" of liberal, Marxist, socialist, and radical (occasionally supplemented by psychoanalytic and existential) have become increasingly inaccurate descriptions of divisions within feminism and fail to exhaust the range of theoretical positions. Some textbook writers attempted to correct the growing problem by tacking on chapters on postmodern feminism and black (or women of color or Third World) feminisms. Even Harding's alternative categorization of empiricist, standpoint, and postmodern has been increasingly blurred (Hekman 1997, 357).[1] Without 25 years of immersion in this rapidly changing field or familiarity with the disputes within the women's movement that have spawned the theoretical debates, students entering this discourse in the late 1990s are at a conceptual disadvantage. Some may enter the field with partial and often distorted understandings of their predecessors as well as different political problems and theoretical concerns. While a discussion about how to teach feminist theory and what constitutes the feminist theory canon is beyond the scope of this short essay (although it would make a fascinating special issue for a feminist journal), my point is merely to relate that what first drew me to this project was a concern about pedagogy and this perspective influenced how I approached the submissions for this issue.

While I attended the 1994 panel with a desire to learn as well as to improve my teaching, I was also concerned about the intersection of political science and women's studies. As a reader of if not contributor to feminist theory, I had often felt that political scientists in general (with the exception of some political theorists) were often marginalized in the interdisciplinary debates within feminist theory. It appeared to me that few political scientists' work had graced the pages of feminist theory texts or interdisciplinary feminist journals,[2] and that few feminist scholars outside the discipline routinely perused the pages of *Women & Politics*. In my view, political scientists had to walk farther across the bridge to participate in interdisciplinary women's studies conversations. It was in part my desire for political science to claim more space within women's studies that led me to lean over during the roundtable and say to Christine di Stefano: "*Women & Politics* should be publishing these papers."[3] Three years later, here they are.

The two concerns that led me to the panel–a desire to ameliorate the confusion of my feminist theory students who encountered standpoint theory and my desire for feminist political science to claim a larger space within women's studies–are indicative of a larger more intractable issue: the difficulties in producing truly interdisciplinary scholarship. Of the commentators on Susan Hekman's article in *Signs,* three argue that those who have appropriated or criticized their work fail to understand it in its proper context. Hartsock argues that her work is too frequently ripped from its roots in Marxist materialist thought. Collins argues that Hekman has abstracted the black feminist standpoint from the context of struggles for social change, particularly, the women's movement. And Smith argues that Hekman fails utterly to appreciate the disciplinary context of Sociology from which her work arises. Students and scholars' misreadings are often a result of their failure to comprehend the specific body of work a feminist theorist is engaged with in her disciplinary subfield as well as within feminist scholarship. All four papers in this volume attempt to place Hartsock and other standpoint theorists in their appropriate historical, theoretical, and political contexts.

I have no panacea for how we will all keep abreast of this burgeoning body of feminist theory scholarship that grows ever more sophisticated and permeates more and more of the disciplines and disciplinary subfields. (Who would have predicted that International Relations, Geography, or Economics would be the exciting feminist growth areas in the 1990s?) Despite the difficulty of the task of mastering two or more disciplines and their feminist intersections, it seems to me that at least two possible responses are undesirable. Either women's studies could wall itself off from the disciplines and construct itself as a separate discipline with participants speaking primarily to each other, or feminist scholars could simply bask in the pleasure of interacting primarily with a very small feminist contingent of their own disciplinary subfield.

In my view, the interaction, exchange, and cross fertilization that results from feminist scholars encountering similar intellectual puzzles in different disciplinary locations and sharing their ideas with each other has invigorated our work. The drawback of this it seems, as the *Signs* entries attest, is that we will more often than not feel misunderstood or misread rather than simply disagreed with. This was certainly the case even among the political scientists on the panel in 1994. And indeed, most of the four papers in this issue direct readers how to interpret Hartsock, lamenting and criticizing what they perceive to be misinterpretations. This special issue takes one step towards opening the conversation about the meaning, interpretation, relevance, and flaws of feminist standpoint theory.

In reading the submissions, my co-editor Helen Kinsella and I were especially intrigued by several submissions that applied feminist standpoint theory to a specific issue. Katherine Welton begins her paper with the observation that Hartsock has moved away from what she calls a "content-centered feminist epistemology." An important part of *Money, Sex, and Power* was specifying the content of the feminist standpoint. We would have liked to publish a paper that applied standpoint theory to a particular case. Yet many of the papers that sought to apply the theory misread Hartsock. If those who write on standpoint theory focus on asserting its existence rather than specifying its content, and if attempts to specify the content seem *prima facie* to be unsatisfactory, does that not say something significant about the theory itself?

All four of the papers, like Hartsock's work, move away from the stark singularity of the feminist standpoint articulated in the early 1980s. All four papers grapple with the frequent and significant arguments levelled against standpoint theorists, weigh them, and come to different conclusions. What is too easily missed by classifying feminists into brands, or following well-publicized disputes between individual feminist theorists, is the extent to which feminist theorists borrow from one another. Fifteen years ago, socialist feminists, for example, attempted to weave together Marxism and radical feminism. Today, I would argue, many standpoint or materialist feminists have learned much from postmodern feminist scholarship. This is not to argue that a happy synthesis is possible, or even that a singular feminist theory is a worth aspiration; rather, it is to draw attention to the constant exchange and synthesis which marks our work. Pigeonholing feminists into categories often neglects exactly this evolution, complexity, and synthesis. The four authors in this volume classify standpoint theory differently, emphasizing its empiricist or its postmodernist tendencies. All four authors are committed to an intellectual debate without creating "straw feminists." All find value in exploring the literature and questions feminist standpoint theory raises, and all plot its evolution.

Although this special issue lists only two co-editors, we were assisted by a group of people at the University of Minnesota with whom we shared and refined our ideas and evaluations. At first, we convened as a group weekly to read and discuss feminist standpoint theories. Later, as the papers came in, we met weekly to discuss them. Carol Chomsky, Oriane Casale, Ann Betzner, Kimberly Simmons, Nathan Dick, Helen Kinsella, and I met regularly. Kathy Reeves, Jane Gilgun, Sonita Sarker, Carol Horton, Christina Rolin, Kira Dahlk, and Heidi Howarth were more occasional participants. Finally, we were greatly assisted by two to four anonymous reviewers of each manuscript.

The co-editor, Helen Kinsella, a Master's student at the Humphrey Institute when the project began and currently enrolled as a doctoral student in Political Science at the University of Minnesota, participated in all of the background reading group discussions, read and reviewed all 25 plus papers, and participated equally in all editorial decisions. My special thanks to Helen, the participants in our reading group, and the support staff of the Humphrey Institute. A special mention is due also to Linda Wagner, the assistant editor of *Women & Politics,* who took over this project after we had started and did a wonderful job.

The pedagogical issues that originally led me to the panel are no longer as pressing for me personally. I no longer teach feminist theory. Many of the insights of feminist standpoint theory, however, are surprisingly relevant to my project of teaching against the dominant paradigm of public policy schools namely, microeconomics. The insights of feminist standpoint theory on the fundamental questions of how group and individual identity is socially constructed and continually produced (rather than presented or discovered as pre-formed, fixed, individual preferences), of how location, interest, and identity combine with political struggle to produce consciousness and the demand for social change, and how experience, location, identity, and power matter for the production of knowledge are all relevant to the study of and practice of public affairs, whether we call the insights "new institutionalism" in political science or economics, or feminist theory. Like the authors of the four papers, I continue to find much of value in feminist standpoint theories.

NOTES

1. Kathy Ferguson offers an alternative and very illuminating distinction between strains of feminist thought in *Signs* 16:2 (1991).

2. Studying the breakdown of disciplines represented in women's studies journals would be an interesting research project. See Kenney, "Women, Feminism, Gender and the Law: Ruminations of a Feminist Academic," *Women & Politics* 15:3 (1995).

3. *Women & Politics* has published a number of significant papers in feminist theory. For example, in 1987, Maria Falco edited a special issue of *Women & Politics* on feminist epistemologies.

REFERENCE

Hekman, Susan. 1997. "Truth and Method: Feminist Standpoint Theory Revisited." *Signs* 22(2): 341-365.

Nancy Hartsock's Standpoint Theory: From Content to "Concrete Multiplicity"

Katherine Welton

This article examines a shift in Nancy Hartsock's theorizing of feminist standpoint epistemology. Hartsock's work has moved from outlining the substantive content and difference of the feminist perspective, based upon the shared character of women's experience, to a more formal understanding of the functioning of a standpoint, without emphasis on the actual content of this perspective. I argue that this shift is a reflection of the wider concerns in feminist theory with the problem of claiming a privileged perspective based upon the collective nature of women's experience. As such, it concerns both the debate over the use of the concept of experience in feminist theory and the issue of differences between women.

I begin by outlining the basis of Hartsock's original development of standpoint theory, from Marxist methodology, in *Money, Sex and Power* (1983). In this I emphasize the role of "experience" in Hartsock's outline of the feminist standpoint. I then discuss the use of experience as a foundational concept in feminist epistemology and the feminist critique of this use. I suggest that this critique can be separated into two strands. The first strand is critical of the way the concept of experience is used to ground feminist epistemology, and the second critique stresses the differences in women's experience rather than the communalities. Hartsock (1990a, 1990b) herself has signalled this concern with differences between women in her later work.

I would like to thank the three anonymous reviewers at *Women & Politics,* and also Sally J. Kenney and Helen Kinsella, for their comments on early drafts of this paper.

[Haworth co-indexing entry note]: "Nancy Hartsock's Standpoint Theory: From Content to 'Concrete Multiplicity.'" Welton, Katherine. Co-published simultaneously in *Women & Politics* (The Haworth Press, Inc.) Vol. 18, No. 3, 1997, pp. 7-24; and: *Politics and Feminist Standpoint Theories* (ed: Sally J. Kenney and Helen Kinsella) The Haworth Press, Inc., 1997, pp. 7-24. Single or multiple copies of this article are available for a fee from The Haworth Document Delivery Service [1-800-342-9678, 9:00 a.m. - 5:00 p.m. (EST). E-mail address: getinfo@haworth.com].

I maintain that, as a response to this concern, Hartsock has effectively "emptied out" the notion of the feminist standpoint. In other words, while retaining the idea of situated knowledge, Hartsock now has moved away from outlining the actual content of the feminist standpoint and how this perspective differs substantively from a masculine world-view. Instead, her work now focuses on the idea it is not a single privileged perspective, but the interplay between different perspectives, that gives us the best kind of knowledge. In an article on feminism and postmodernism, Hartsock (1990a, 171) argued that we need to "dissolve the false 'we' I have been using into its real multiplicity and variety and out of this concrete multiplicity build an account of the world as seen from the margins." This "slide" away from identifying the content of the singular feminist standpoint toward multiplicity has occurred in several feminist approaches to epistemology, both standpoint and postmodern.[1] I argue that this move is largely reflective of growing reservations about the way in which the concept of experience is used in the construction of the feminist standpoint.

The consequences of this retreat from content and emphasis on the diverse and situated nature of knowledge production brings with it some interesting problems for feminist theory and practice. Not least is the issue of how to construct adequate feminist knowledge. Donna Haraway (1983) has argued that "scientific debate is a contest for the language to announce what will count as public knowledge . . . Feminism, like science, is a myth, a contest for public knowledge" (176). In other words, without foundationalist concepts such as truth or objectivity upon which to ground knowledge, epistemological issues are increasingly bound up in the political contestations that shape the production of knowledge. In a recent symposium on feminist standpoint theory, Hartsock addresses the complicated relationship between the political and epistemological claims of standpoint theory. The political significance of standpoint rests on its claim to represent marginalized knowledges, while the epistemological force emerges from the standpoint claim to a privileged view of reality. Although Hartsock (1997, 373) refers briefly to the choice between "truth" or "justice" in the title of the piece, it is clear that she regards it as a false choice, as there are no clear distinctions to be made between the political and the epistemological role of the feminist standpoint.

The intersection of "truth and justice" is highly significant for feminist theory, not only because the contest for public knowledge occurs in a wider, non-feminist arena but also occurs within feminism itself. The problems associated with the project of identifying and articulating a single feminist standpoint are dramatically intensified when we admit the possibility of a variety of feminist standpoints, some overlapping, some conflicting, yet all constitutive of each other in various ways. This is the beginning point of Hartsock's "concrete multiplicity," yet Hartsock does not discuss the kinds of procedures, institutions, or models of organization that feminist theory might adopt in order to access and accommodate a variety of differing standpoints beyond a blanket statement that such an accommodation is necessary. In conclusion, therefore, I will examine some potential problems with building such a "concrete multiplicity."

HARTSOCK'S STANDPOINT THEORY

Hartsock's original formulation of the feminist standpoint, in *Money, Sex and Power* (1983), should be read within the context of the "unhappy marriage" debate.[2] This debate occurred mostly in the late '70s and early '80s, and was concerned with the failure to adequately theorize the relationship between Marxism and feminism. It is this debate that shapes Hartsock's fundamental research problem, namely, the gap in Marxist understandings of race and sex and the ways in which these systems of domination influence class. What Hartsock borrows from Marxist methodology is her emphasis on praxis: the ontological and constitutive character of labor, and the concept of the standpoint.

Hartsock defines praxis as the idea that "one can only know and appropriate the world (change it and be changed by it) through practical activity" (95). As Hartsock herself acknowledges, "the concept of a standpoint depends on the assumption that epistemology grows in a complex and contradictory way from material life" (117). What this means in bald epistemological terms is that human productive activity will structure human knowledge. For example, Hartsock argues that the activity of the capitalist, namely commodity exchange, serves to structure capitalist understanding of the world; therefore, market or exchange models of social organization will necessarily reflect a capitalist world view.

In addition to this response to Marxist theory, Hartsock's early formulation of the feminist standpoint is also concerned with retheorizing power from a feminist perspective. For Hartsock, power is an important concept because it can provide a legitimate basis of organizing communities and community action. She argues that "to examine these theories of power is to involve oneself in the questions of how communities have been constructed, how they have been legitimized and how they might be structured in more liberatory ways" (1983, 4). Hartsock examines the ways in which we presently understand power, identifying what she sees as a lack of "theoretical clarity about how these relations of domination are constructed, how they operate, and how social theories and practices have both justified and obscured them" (1). She questions whether present conceptions of power might be understood as masculine and suggests that we might come to understand power a little better by an approach that includes the previously neglected resource of women's lived experience. Hartsock emphasizes the need to examine women's lived experience, because she argues that each theory of power rests on a different ontology and epistemology, thus broader feminist reappraisals of these issues will have consequences for theories of power.

In light of these consequences, any proper examination of theories of power, Hartsock argues, must also include a consideration of the relation of knowledge to human activity and the relations between knowledge and domination. Within Marxist epistemology, our knowledge and the perspective from which we view the world are both structured by production and by the labor that we perform. As a result, capital and labor will have a different perspective; they will literally see the world in different ways. However, as Hartsock (1983, 149) points out, the gender bias in Marxist thought ignores the fact that these categories will be masculine and feminine as well because of differences in women's role in production and reproduction.

For Hartsock, the basis for an alternative, specifically feminist understanding of power emerges from the possibility that "women's experience of power relations, and thus their understanding, may be importantly and structurally different from the lives and therefore the theories of men" (151). Hartsock uses women's experience to critique the epistemological and ontological basis of traditional theories of power and economic organization. Hartsock claims that the economic models blithely assume that human nature equals "rational economic man," but there is no inherent reason to think that this is an accurate portrayal of human nature. On the contrary, she argues that "one could begin to see the outline of a very different type of community if one took the mother/infant relation rather than market exchange as the prototypic human interaction" (42).

Women's experience (mediated by a feminist politics–an essential point to which I will return later) provides an alternative view of reality because of the sexual division of labor. That is, "much of the work involved in reproducing labor power is done by women, and . . . much of the male worker's contact with nature outside the factory is mediated by women" (Hartsock 1983, 234). Hartsock is not interested in individual exceptions to this rule because structurally, she argues, there still remains overwhelmingly a sexual division of labor. Whether or not individual women conform in terms of their everyday activities does not, for Hartsock, alter the fact that "women as a sex are institutionally responsible for producing both goods and human beings" (234).

The main difference that Hartsock establishes between the labor of men and that of women is that the nature of women's work, both publicly and in the private sphere, submerges women "in the world of use–in concrete, many qualitied, changing material processes" (235), in a much more comprehensive way than the labor of men. For Hartsock, if we accept the argument that the work we do shapes our material existence and epistemological perspective, then the substantive difference of women's work, in its very concreteness and grounded nature, grants women a uniquely privileged standpoint position from which to view the world.

The existence of an alternative standpoint does not entail, however, that the master's perspective can simply be ignored, even if it can be shown to be partial and perverse. In other words, the experience of the dominant group is never simply false or wrong. As Hartsock (1983) argues, in reference to pornography, "this experience, because of the hegemony of that group, sets the dynamics of the social relations in which all parties are forced to participate–women as well as men, unmasculine as well as masculine men" (178).

The experience and perspective of the dominant group, therefore, should not simply be dismissed as wrong. What this means for the feminist standpoint is that there must be an active, political resistance to work against the material embodiment of the perspective and experience of the dominant group. It is the act of having to push against the experience-made-reality of the hegemonic group, that makes it a political standpoint and potentially liberating.

This claim obviously goes beyond a simple call for a recognition of the situated nature of knowledge production. It is a claim for privileged knowledge production and for the emancipatory character of the knowledge that is produced. Hartsock claims that the feminist standpoint "not only makes available a privileged vantage point on social relations but also points beyond those relations in more liberatory directions" (1983, 226). Hartsock does not refer to it as a "women's standpoint" but rather as a "feminist standpoint," thus reiterating the political nature of the standpoint and the fact that it must be achieved and that it has a "liberatory potential." This is central, as Hartsock argues, because the material activities that women perform are not in themselves inherently radical, or insightful; for Hartsock, "women's experience and activity as a dominated group contains both negative and positive aspects" (232).

What emerges from Hartsock's early formulation of standpoint epistemology is a definite sense of the substantive, actual difference in men's and women's perspective. She says of the male standpoint that:

> masculine experience when replicated as epistemology leads to a world conceived as (and in fact) inhabited by a number of fundamentally hostile others whom one comes to know by means of opposition (even death struggle) and yet with whom one must construct a social relation in order to survive. (1983, 242)

In contrast to this rather bleak portrayal, Hartsock describes mediated women's experience as almost directly opposite. The feminist perspective opposes "dualisms of any sort; [and involves a] valuation of concrete, everyday life; a sense of a variety of connectednesses and continuities both with other persons and with the natural world" (242).

This emphasis on the substantive content of the feminist standpoint appears again with Hartsock's characterization of feminist retheorization of power as not domination, "but as capacity, on power as a capacity of the community as a whole" (253). For Hartsock this means that "women's experience of connection and relation have consequences for understandings of power and may hold resources for a more liberatory understanding" (253). It is precisely this nomination of substantive content of a feminist epistemology, however, and its attendant reliance on the concept of women's lived experience, that is problematic for feminist knowledge production.

One problem, identified by Judith Grant (1993), lies in Hartsock's use of theories of power developed by female theorists such as Hannah Arendt, Hanna Pitkin, and Dorothy Emmet, to provide specific models with which to contrast what she sees as traditional (masculine) understandings of power with alternative views of power. Hartsock argues that these alternatives from female theorists, who would not call themselves feminists, are remarkably similar to more explicitly feminist approaches to power. Hartsock is unwilling to state that there is anything more than "suggestive evidence" for this similarity (1983, 210). Nevertheless, it is an example of a substantive claim about the content and character of the feminist standpoint. As I argue later, it is this kind of substantive claim that is absent from her later reworking of standpoint theory because of concerns with the exclusionary and essentialist nature of these kinds of claims.

Grant (1993, 117) argues that Hartsock's references to these (non-feminist) communitarian theorists are problematic because any difference in their understandings of power may be better explained by political inclination rather than a specifically female perspective. Grant's critique illustrates some of the problems with identifying explicitly the content of the difference of the feminist perspective. Such problems may help in part to explain Hartsock's shift to a position that does not identify the explicit difference of the feminist perspective.

I suggest that Hartsock's shift from a clear delineation of the actual difference of the feminist standpoint to a more general argument about the need for multiple standpoints (or "concrete multiplicity") comes from the critiques of the concept of women's experience as it is used in feminist epistemology and theory. In the next section of this paper, I outline these critiques and suggest where Hartsock's position has altered to reflect these challenges.

Experience in Feminist Epistemology

Feminist theory has been engaged in a reappraisal of the concept of experience that has been the basis of much of its epistemology and political practice.[3] The criticism of the role of women's experience in epistemology, I argue, takes the form of two discrete elements that are in some ways connected but that are more fruitfully talked about separately. The first is a critique of the epistemological or foundational status of "experience" in feminist theory, and the second is a critique of the exclusive nature of the experiences that have been articulated up until now.

The epistemological critique of the use of the concept of experience emerges from the problematic relationship between women's lived experience and the construction of the feminist standpoint. Experience is not innocent, as Donna Haraway (1990, 240) suggests, "we must struggle over the terms of its articulation." In some feminist theory, experience is assigned the role of the foundation of knowledge, and as Scott (1992, 25) argues "the vision of the individual subject . . . becomes the bedrock of evidence upon which explanation is built." The effect of this is to ignore the constructive function of language, discourse, and history thus taking meaning to be transparent. Grosz (1993, 40) also questions the "rather naive views of experience" that have taken it as ". . . the unquestionable and final arbiter in disputes, seeing in it access to a pure femininity or some kind of incontrovertible truth." This reconsideration of the status of women's experience complicates the idea of the feminist standpoint, as it serves to question the very foundation upon which it is based.

Part of the problem with the use of the concept of experience is that it is vulnerable to being used in a fundamentally conservative manner. Gallop (1983) argues that experience, which she also refers to as "simple referentiality," can only be the basis of a politically conservative politics. When women's experience is taken as authentic without further examination of its relationship to what Gallop calls "traditional ideological constructs" (83), then the result will reflect this conservative approach.

This same critique is a feature of the debates around the question of objective versus subjective interests (e.g., Jonasdottir 1988). Some feminists stress the need to develop a concept of objective interests to avoid the conservatism of an epistemology or political practice based entirely on women's subjective interests, in other words, only those interests which they themselves identify as their own, arguably a consequence of focussing on lived experience. The problem of experience still remains however, in the question of how these interests will be identified. If it is not to be an entirely arbitrary process, then some reference to women's experiences is still surely necessary. In an early article written with Irene Diamond (1981), Hartsock suggests that the narrow understanding of women as just another interest group does not touch on the unique perspective that emerges from the concrete difference in men's and women's life activity. This is an important precursor to her later work on justifying the grounds for the feminist standpoint.

In *Money, Sex and Power* (1983), Hartsock does not rely on the naive conceptions of women's experience that the above authors seek to criticize. For Hartsock, a feminist standpoint is essential as the catalyst to the raw material of experience, in that it "picks out and amplifies the liberatory possibilities contained in that experience" (232). The feminist perspective does not consist only of the unformed data provided by women's lived experience. In Hartsock's epistemology, a standpoint is achieved, not directly given; it is a "mediated rather than immediate understanding" (132). Nonetheless, this still does not really address the problem of experience in epistemological terms largely because this process of interpreting and shaping raw experience is never clearly described. As Hennessy (1993) suggests, one of the problems with the argument that the standpoint is achieved, not simply a reiteration of the basic experience of women's lives, is that there is a failure to adequately explain the movement "between the discursive materiality of feminism and the empirical materiality of women's lives" (67).

That this relationship between empirical experience and feminist interpretation is not adequately conceptualized signals one of the main problems in Hartsock's work and in standpoint theory more generally. It is never made precisely clear just how the selection and amplification of emancipatory aspects of women's experience translates to the actual feminist standpoint. The role of the feminist academic, for example, should be examined more closely, as they are in some way responsible for interpreting women's experience and for mediating between women's lived experience and the feminist standpoint. There is no clear examination of this role in Hartsock's work.[4]

I have argued that Hartsock's shift toward multiple standpoints can be understood as a reaction to the criticisms of essentialism that face the earlier formulations of the distinctive character of the feminist standpoint. Even if this is the case, such a shift does not circumvent the inadequacy of standpoint theorists' formulations of the movement between experience and standpoint. If anything, arguing that knowledge must emerge from multiple, partial perspectives would seem to exacerbate this problem because of the need to interpret more than one perspective. I return to this point in the final section of my paper in which I discuss some possible problems with accommodating multiple standpoints to produce better knowledge.

DIFFERENCE AND THE FEMINIST STANDPOINT

In addition to the specifically epistemological challenge, the feminist use of the concept of experience has also undergone a challenge based upon differences between women. I identify these two challenges to experience as separate. In reality, however, both the reaction against experience as a foundationalist concept and the recognition of the challenge posed by the differences between women's experiences tend to be interrelated. I have chosen to demarcate them because this illustrates some important differences of focus in the two critiques. To do so also allows the possibility that one might want to concern oneself with differences between women without a subsequent abandonment of foundationalist concepts or, conversely, that one might happily abandon foundations without being particularly receptive to an assertion of the importance of multiplicity. To identify this critique as separate from the epistemological critique also avoids what seems to be the paradox of criticizing "experience" (epistemologically) by using the evidence of the lived experience of women's difference from other women.

The assertion of the differences in women's experiences questions the idea that women share sufficiently common experience to identify a single set of common interests or one single communal standpoint. Attempts to do so deny differences between women, in such a way that the experience of the dominant group, in this case, western, white, middle-class women, is taken to represent the experience of women as a whole. This second critique comes from black women and other women of color, lesbians, and women from non-Western nations, among others, who argue that their own experiences have been excluded from feminist theory in much the same way that feminists first argued that women's experiences were not properly articulated within Western male political theory. This critique suggests that the much vaunted "experience" in feminist thought is in fact the experience of white, Western, middle-class, heterosexual women. Some recent examples of this critique, specifically relating to epistemological issues, include the work of black feminists such as bell hooks (1990) and Patricia Hill Collins (1996), also work from other women of color such as Chandra Talpade Mohanty (1987) and Uma Narayan (1989), and from theorists of the lesbian perspective, such as Julia Penelope (1990) and Joyce Trebilcot (1990).

This critique does not involve a necessary challenge to the epistemological foundations of feminist theory. As Harvey (1989) argues, the incorporation of different voices, or different standpoints, in other words, the recognition of differences between women, is at least nominally compatible with feminist standpoint theory. It need not mean total subjectivity and relativism, anti-foundationalism, or infinite standpoints. In other words, at one level, standpoint theory can accommodate the idea of multiple feminist perspectives. What it is demonstrably not compatible with, however, is an insistence on the particular character of a singular feminist standpoint, as Hartsock outlined over a decade ago. Hartsock was then insistent that the relatively universally shared experience of women's productive and reproductive role constituted a sufficient communality to overcome differences of race, class, and sexuality.

While signalling her awareness of the problem of denying the difference of the experiences of women of color and lesbians, for example, Hartsock (1983) still stressed that "the effort to uncover a feminist standpoint assumes that there are some things common to all women's lives in Western class societies" (234). In response to objections to the attempt to construct communalities between women across race and class barriers, Hartsock (233) argued that she took some justification from Marx in doing so because Marx ignored differences between men, such as country of origin, ethnicity, and race when constructing his own model of social relations.

This is not exactly satisfactory, and Hartsock's approach was criticized for this rather cavalier dismissal of the differences between women. Crosby, for example, is critical of this aspect of Hartsock's work. Crosby (1992, 137) is also critical of feminist standpoint theory because it assumes that "ontology is the ground of epistemology, that who I am determines what and how I know." In other words, despite its purported materialist basis, Crosby sees essentialist tendencies in feminist standpoint theory.

It seems a little harsh, however, to read Hartsock's original formulation of standpoint theory as a simple kind of essentialism or ontological determinism. Hartsock's standpoint theory was not grounded in an essentialized conception of womankind but rather in the epistemological significance of shared life experiences, common to women on materialist grounds, but not innately essential to them. Women, in Hartsock's standpoint theory, were seen to possess a material and epistemological difference rather than an essential difference. This is by no means the rank essentialism of a biological determinist claim. What is problematic, however, about Hartsock's original formulation of the feminist standpoint is that Hartsock nominates the substantive content of the feminist standpoint, not just the methodological basis for it. This substantive content was based upon experiences of productive activity that she argues were structurally common to Western women. Hartsock is arguably justified in suggesting that these activities are still by overwhelming majority the responsibility of women. Nonetheless, there are significant material differences between women that underlie a general statement that women as a whole are still largely responsible for the labor of the private sphere. Working-class women and women of color, for example, perform a disproportionate share of the actual labor of the private sphere in Western capitalist society. In such cases it is clear that although the "responsibility" of the labor of the private sphere may still be regarded as women's preserve, the actual work that is performed cannot be said to rest equally with all women. Furthermore, even where there are common experiences, these will have different effects and be interpreted differently, according to a variety of factors, including the class and race, of the subjects involved. The meaning and interpretation of women's experiences, both common and diverse, does not have the transparency assumed in some ways by Hartsock's original account of the content of the feminist standpoint and method of attaining it.

Hartsock has recognized the epistemological significance of differences between women in her more recent work and has shifted from a focus on a single feminist standpoint to the idea that better feminist accounts of the world emerge from the interplay of multiple perspectives, or "concrete multiplicity" (1990a, 171). Despite this recognition, she does continue to argue that "at the level of epistemology there are a number of similarities that can provide the basis for differing groups to understand each other and form alliances" (1990b, 31). What has changed from earlier work is that there is now a reluctance to nominate the content of any particular standpoint and a move toward multiplicity of perspectives as a means toward better knowledge production.

This shift is significant for a number of reasons. It constitutes, for example, a distinct break with other standpoint claims for an explicitly female "voice" that were often based upon essentialist assumptions about women and, in particular, the mother/child relationship.[5] As such, it represents a move away from what might be called a version of the "equality/difference" dilemma as it appears in feminist epistemology. Because Hartsock maintains the idea that the visions of the oppressed do give a privileged perspective, her position cannot be categorized as an equality one, in the sense that all perspectives are seen as equally valid. Nonetheless, her later reluctance to nominate the actual content of the feminist perspective also moves away from a claim that we can know and articulate women's difference. Although she does not explicitly say so, Hartsock's later position seems more open to a conception of women's perspectives and interests as changing and strategic.

The move toward multiple perspectives is also significant because it may indicate common ground between standpoint and postmodern feminists. Despite remaining critical of what she sees as the epistemological and political shortcomings of postmodernism, Hartsock herself suggests that this shift is a reflection upon the perceived usefulness of postmodernism for feminist theory, in particular "arguments about incommensurability, multiplicity, and the lack of definitive answers" (1990b, 16). Even though Hartsock ultimately rejects the possibility of a politically viable postmodern feminism, her later position shares with many feminist postmodernists a desire to include more voices and perspectives in the process of producing knowledge.

Above all, it is this response to the criticism of exclusion that constitutes the main significance of the shift in Hartsock's work. The new focus on multiplicity is grounded in the idea that diverse perspectives, feminist and otherwise, are the only way to get a better account of the world. This shift in emphasis has the potential to enrich and diversify the process of feminist knowledge production, paradoxically, in its very refusal to nominate the specific character and content of the feminist standpoint. Unfortunately, Hartsock does not discuss in any concrete way the possibilities in terms of formal procedures or political practices that might enable multiple standpoints to contest meanings and produce knowledge. In the final section, I consider briefly some moves toward such theory in feminist epistemology and conclude with some of the pertinent issues that face a fully inclusive, or perhaps democratic, production of knowledge.

ACCOMMODATING DIFFERENCE: STANDPOINT THEORY AND DEMOCRACY

The challenge to the epistemological status of women's experience and the challenge raised by the potential diversity of multiple feminist perspectives, both raise questions about the legitimate organization of knowledge producing communities. As I claimed earlier, Hartsock's rationale for her original work on feminist standpoint theory lay in part with its usefulness for understanding the relationships between power, communities, and gender. The articulation of a feminist standpoint, Hartsock argued (1983, 247), "would raise, for the first time in human history, the possibility of a fully human community, a community structured by a variety of connections rather than separation and opposition." For Hartsock, therefore, the retheorization of power, via the vehicle of the feminist standpoint, can lead to new understandings of the legitimate organization of communities.

Hartsock calls, in her later work, for feminists to build a "concrete multiplicity" of perspectives as a means to gain a better understanding of the world from the standpoints of marginal subjects. The concept of a "concrete multiplicity" seems to incorporate the idea that knowledge production is a communal activity.[6] Nevertheless, the specific nature of this kind of community remains undertheorized in Hartsock's work. The most obvious question concerns the kind of procedural arrangements or, more simply, the political principles of organization around which to structure the communal production of knowledge. While Hartsock has acknowledged the value of multiple perspectives in her more recent work, there is little indication of what it might mean to try and build a "concrete multiplicity" in practice.

This critique should not be read simply as a call for feminist theorists to state more clearly the kind of procedural and institutional reforms necessary to undertake a communal approach to knowledge production. That in itself is a worthwhile task but one which would first require some clarification, as there are some further problems with the idea that the best kind of knowledge might emerge out of the interplay of multiple perspectives.

One problem lies with the question of whether standpoints can change significantly. As I have argued, Hartsock's original theory of the feminist standpoint ascribed a fixed content to it, but in her later work, this is absent. Nevertheless, there is still no consideration of how standpoints themselves might be transformed by the intersubjective process that would seem to be entailed by the idea of a "concrete multiplicity." We cannot assume, for example, that the process of contestation for the right to articulate public knowledge will not alter or change that knowledge in some way. Hartsock does not consider the effect that building democratic, diverse knowledge production would have upon the construction and maintenance of standpoints themselves. This would entail a much more detailed understanding of the operation of a diverse, intersubjective knowledge producing community than has so far been the case.

Some feminist theorists, most consistently Sandra Harding (1991, 151) in her work on reconceptualizing objectivity, have suggested that this should be democratic, but there is little substantial treatment in Harding's work of what it might actually mean to democratically organize the communal production of knowledge. This is a significant oversight, given the impetus within much feminist epistemology to expand the concept of representation to include multiple feminist perspectives.

Perhaps one way of beginning this kind of project is to clarify what exactly is meant by the use of concepts such as democracy particularly when such concepts are put forward as solutions to epistemological problems. To blithely borrow models from democratic theory will not serve the purpose. Nonetheless, feminist work in other areas of democracy and representation might provide insights into the treatment of the issues of diversity and participation that could be incorporated into epistemological frameworks.

To illustrate this, I have used the example of Iris Marion Young's work on the representation of difference within democracy. Young suggests that we need to establish recognized procedures to facilitate the inclusion of marginalized groups. She argues that "a democratic public, however that is constituted, should provide mechanisms for the effective representation and recognition of the distinct voices and perspectives of those of its constituent groups that are oppressed or disadvantaged within it" (1990, 124). These aids to participation, Young suggests, should only be specifically for the purpose of representing those presently oppressed or marginalized, as our democracies already provide sufficient representation for dominant groups (124). Young suggests that this kind of approach to representation can help to uncover the universalization of the experiences of a dominant group.

Mouffe (1992, 381) questions whether Young's model of public contestation would, in practice degenerate into "a political process of hegemonic articulation, and not simply . . . free and undistorted communication." The implication is that in a contest of differing perspectives, pluralism without established commitments to shared goals will lead only to a reassertion of the dominant paradigm. Young's solution to this problem is to establish procedural grounds upon which some perspectives would be privileged over others in certain circumstances. This kind of proposal for the representation of difference might work, but as Mouffe (1992) argues, it tends to assume that standpoint identities or positions are already fully constituted prior to the process of public contestation. This raises again the problem of how the process of democratic contestation, or democratic consensus building, might alter standpoints themselves. In

Hartsock's version of "concrete multiplicity," there is no acknowledgment of the role that the process of debate and adjudication might play in the construction of situated knowledge, and the formation of standpoint identities.

Another issue that flows from this is the developmental aspect of any kind of procedural mechanism for participation in the construction of knowledge. Not all people have equal participatory skills, and these skills might develop over time, and this development would be embedded in the process of participation itself. It would follow from this that identities and standpoints could not participate in the construction of public knowledge and remain fixed or immutable. If this fixed character is assumed, then this enshrines these standpoints as always oppressed and positions them as always alternative and marginal. The model of "concrete multiplicity" should, therefore, also include some consideration of the developmental possibilities that participation might bring.

Any model based upon multiplicity must also deal with conflicts of interpretation that might arise from different feminist standpoints. While it is true that feminist standpoint theory can theoretically accommodate multiple standpoints, the means for dealing with conflicting, or even infinite standpoints, are not so clear. As it stands, the idea of a more inclusive and democratic means of knowledge production avoids the issue of the existence of winners and losers in any contest of meaning. In doing so, it seems to rely on an assumption of consensus that might truncate opportunities for genuine participation or substitute a false imposition of consensus in place of a genuine multiplicity.

The final problem with the establishment of a "concrete multiplicity" lies with the problems posed by women's continuing work commitments in the private sphere. Despite the recognition from within standpoint theory of the epistemological significance of this role, there is little real consideration of how these commitments construct barriers against women's full participation in the public sphere. The question of what institutional mechanisms would ensure the full participation of women, and other oppressed groups, must also be accompanied by a reappraisal of what institutions prevent these groups from participating effectively at present.

This is only a brief examination of some of the problems facing the idea that the best kind of knowledge is the product of a community of multiple perspectives. As such, it has done little more than indicate the extent of work needed to make feminist knowledge production properly representative of the diverse experiences and needs of women. Hartsock's contribution to this project lies not so much in her early assertion of the content of the feminist standpoint but in her articulation of the ways in which marginalized groups can claim a privileged perspective on reality and the urgent character of this enterprise. The shift in focus from a content-centered single feminist standpoint to the interplay between differing feminist perspectives highlights the political stakes that operate within claims for public knowledge. While the new political claims do place unfamiliar pressures on the construction of feminist knowledge, they simultaneously provide a wider scope for the process of constructing and transforming both our knowledge and reality.

NOTES

1. For example, Sandra Harding's call (1991) for "strong" objectivity; the idea that objective knowledge, in the sense of the best account of the material world, emerges from the interplay between situated knowledge perspectives. See also Donna Haraway (1991, 196), who argues that a larger vision of the world emerges not from the view from nowhere, but from ". . . the joining of partial views and halting voices into a collective subject position."

2. See for example Sargent, ed. 1981.

3. Very briefly, recent examples of this have included Gallop 1983, Grant 1987, Grosz 1993, Haraway 1990, Harding 1991, Mohanty 1987, and Scott 1992.

4. For some discussion of the relationship between feminist academics and women's experience, see Patricia Hill Collins (1996) whose essay explores the difficult movement between black women's experience and black feminist thought.

5. Carol Gilligan's work (1982) is the most obvious example of this, although she did not argue that this "different voice" was exclusively female.

6. The idea of knowledge production as a communal activity is not unique to Hartsock or even unique to feminist theory. Some feminists who have explored the idea of communal knowledge production as a means of accommodating different perspectives include Helen Longino (1993), Lynn Hankinson Nelson (1993), and Sandra Harding (1991). See also note 2 above.

REFERENCES

Collins, Patricia Hill. 1996. "The Social Construction of Black Feminist Thought." In *Women, Knowledge and Reality: Explorations in Feminist Philosophy*, 2nd ed., ed. A. Garry and M. Pearsall. New York: Routledge.

Crosby, Christina. 1992. "Dealing with Differences." In *Feminists Theorize the Political,* ed. J. Butler and J. Scott. New York: Routledge.

Diamond, Irene and Nancy Hartsock. 1981. "Beyond Interests in Politics: A Comment on Virginia Sapiro's "When Are Interests Interesting? The Problem of Political Representation of Women." *American Political Science Review* 75(3):717-721.

Gallop, Jane. 1983. "Quand nos lèvres s'écrivent: Irigaray's Body Politic" [When Our Lips Are Writing Each Other: Irigaray's Body Politic]. *Romantic Review* 74(1):77-83.

Gilligan, Carol. 1982. *In a Different Voice: Psychological Theory and Women's Development.* Cambridge, Mass.: Harvard University Press.

Grant, Judith. 1987. "I Feel Therefore I Am: A Critique of Female Experience as the Basis for a Feminist Epistemology." *Women & Politics* 7(3):99-114.

_____. 1993. *Fundamental Feminism: Contesting the Core Concepts of Feminist Theory.* New York: Routledge.

Grosz, Elizabeth. A. 1993. "Merleau-Ponty and Irigaray in the Flesh." *Thesis Eleven* 36: 37-59.

Haraway, Donna J. 1983. "The Contest for Primate Nature: Daughters of Man-the-Hunter in the Field, 1960-1980." In *The Future of American Democracy: Views from the Left,* ed. Mark E. Kann. Philadelphia: Temple University Press.

_____. 1990. "Reading Buchi Emecheta: Contests for Women's Experience in Women's Studies." *Women: A Cultural Review* 1(3):240-55.

_____. 1991. "Situated Knowledges: The Science Question in Feminism and the Privilege of Partial Perspective." In *Simians, Cyborgs and Women: The Reinvention of Nature,* ed. Donna J. Haraway. New York: Routledge.

Harding, Sandra. 1991. *Whose Science? Whose Knowledge? Thinking from Women's Lives.* Ithaca, New York: Cornell University Press.

Hartsock, Nancy. 1983. *Money, Sex and Power: Toward a Feminist Historical Materialism.* New York: Longman.

_____. 1990a. "Foucault on Power: A Theory for Women?" In *Feminism/Postmodernism,* ed. L. Nicholson. New York:Routledge.

_____. 1990b. "Postmodernism and Political Change: Issues for Feminist Theory." *Cultural Critique* 14:15-33.

_____. 1997. "Comment on Hekman's 'Truth and Method: Feminist Standpoint Theory Revisited': Truth or Justice?" *Signs* 22(2):367-374.

Harvey, Louise. 1989. "The Post-Modernist Turn in Feminist Philosophy of Science." *Arena* 88:119-33.

Hennessy, Rosemary. 1993. *Materialist Feminism and the Politics of Discourse.* New York: Routledge.

hooks, bell. 1990. "Feminism: A Transformational Politic." In *Theoretical Perspectives on Sexual Difference,* ed. D. Rhode. New Haven: Yale University Press.

Jonasdottir, Anna G. 1988. "On the Concept of Interest, Women's Interests, and the Limitations of Interest Theory." In *The Political Interests of Gender,* ed. K. Jones and A. Jonasdottir. London: Sage.

Longino, Helen. 1993. "Subjects, Power and Knowledge: Description and Prescription in Feminist Philosophies of Science." In *Feminist Epistemologies,* ed. L. Alcoff and E. Potter. New York: Routledge.

Mohanty, Chandra Talpade. 1987. "Feminist Encounters: Locating the Politics of Experience." *Copyright* 1:30-44.

Mouffe, Chantal. 1992. "Feminism, Citizenship, and Radical Democratic Politics." In *Feminists Theorize the Political,* ed. J. Butler and J. Scott. New York: Routledge.

Narayan, Uma. 1989. "The Project of Feminist Epistemology: Perspectives from a Nonwestern Feminist." In *Gender/Body/Knowledge: Feminist Reconstructions of Being and Knowing,* ed. A. Jaggar and S. Bordo. New Jersey: Rutgers University.

Nelson, Lynn Hankinson. 1993. "Epistemological Communities." In *Feminist Epistemologies,* ed. L. Alcoff and E. Potter. New York: Routledge.

Penelope, Julia. 1990. "The Lesbian Perspective." In *Lesbian Philosophies and Cultures,* ed. J. Allen. New York: SUNY Press.

Trebilcot, Joyce. 1990. "Dyke Methods." In *Lesbian Philosophies and Cultures,* ed. J. Allen. New York: SUNY Press.

Sargent, Lydia, ed. 1981. *Women and Revolution: A Discussion of the Unhappy Marriage of Marxism and Feminism.* London: Pluto Press.

Scott, Joan W. 1992. "Experience." In *Feminists Theorize the Political,* ed. Judith Butler and Joan W. Scott. New York: Routledge.

Young, Iris M. 1990. "Polity and Group Difference: A Critique of the Ideal of Universal Citizenship." In *Throwing Like a Girl and Other Essays in Feminist Philosophy and Social Theory,* ed. Iris M. Young. Bloomington: Indiana University Press.

Where Standpoint Stands Now

Catherine Hundleby

SUMMARY. I argue, in opposition to recent criticism by Helen Longino and Richmond Campbell, that standpoint theory is needed for a feminist account of knowledge. Its recently emerging empiricist tendencies do not make it redundant and unnecessarily confrontational. Feminist empiricism directs us to seek out different perspectives, and standpoint theory enhances empirical resources by increasing the variety of available perspectives through redressing political marginalization. Standpoint theory aims to counteract the deleterious affects of oppression on the availability of unique resources for knowledge, which cannot be achieved on a strictly empiricist account.

Nancy Hartsock's article "The Feminist Standpoint: Towards a Specifically Feminist Historical Materialism," from the first collection of feminist epistemology, *Discovering Reality* (1983a), is the *locus classicus* of standpoint theory. Since then, however, standpoint theory has metamorphosed such that it is in many ways unrecognizable as Hartsock's approach, and its similarity to the theories known as "feminist empiricism" is increasingly apparent. Standpoint theory is grounded in the materialism of its Marxian origins and so is committed in its inception to a version of empiricism: knowledge depends on experience. More specifically, standpoint theory is increasingly like feminist empiricism in viewing greater experience as enhancing the quality of knowledge. *[Article copies available for a fee from The Haworth Document Delivery Service: 1-800-342-9678. E-mail address: getinfo@haworth.com]*

I would like to thank Alison Wylie, Kathleen Okruhlik, and the Philosophy Graduate Student Symposium at the University of Western Ontario for their enlightening criticisms of an earlier version of this paper, and to thank the editors of this volume for aiding the development of my position by helping me locate the most recent discussions of standpoint theory.

[Haworth co-indexing entry note]: "Where Standpoint Stands Now." Hundleby, Catherine. Co-published simultaneously in *Women & Politics* (The Haworth Press, Inc.) Vol. 18, No. 3, 1997, pp. 25-43; and: *Politics and Feminist Standpoint Theories* (ed: Sally J. Kenney and Helen Kinsella) The Haworth Press, Inc., 1997, pp. 25-43. Single or multiple copies of this article are available for a fee from The Haworth Document Delivery Service [1-800-342-9678, 9:00 a.m. - 5:00 p.m. (EST). E-mail address: getinfo@haworth.com].

Recognizing the emerging continuity of standpoint theory with empiricism, Richmond Campbell (1994) and Helen Longino (1993) have argued that empiricism should be preferred as a theory of knowledge for feminism because it is better supported by traditional epistemology than is the Marxism of standpoint theory. However, Campbell and Longino do not recognize that standpoint theory is a powerful tool to accompany feminist empiricism; it counteracts the oppression that can inhibit the development of empirical resources for knowledge. Empiricism directs people to seek out different perspectives for understanding. Standpoint theory increases the variety of available perspectives by addressing the problem of marginalization, by counteracting the tendency of oppression to limit knowledge. Opposition to oppression enhances empirical resources by giving voice to perspectives that otherwise are inaccessible because they are hidden or undeveloped. Achieving a standpoint requires addressing the uniformity in experiences of oppression. For this reason, it has been argued that standpoints are pernicious in neglecting the differences among women and in reinforcing the social distinctions that underpin different forms of oppression by treating them as reflective of an inner essence (e.g., of women, blacks, lesbians). However, standpoints reveal that specific forms of oppression influence understanding as *contingencies* that are "partial and perverse," in Hartsock's words (1983a, 303). Partiality is unavoidable because knowledge must be situated (Haraway 1991), but confronting the political structure of a particular historical and material partiality helps to reveal perverse circumstances and eliminate them. Without such a strategy, and despite all good intentions, feminist empiricism cannot access perspectives that are politically marginalized: empirical input would not be maximized in a way that counteracts the conservative tendencies of science as a politically central system for acquiring knowledge. Without an alliance with standpoint theory, feminist empiricism is impoverished as an epistemology for feminism.

THE STANDPOINT TRADITION

Hartsock coined the term "feminist standpoint" in her 1983 expansion of some then-recent work by Marxist feminists. This type of approach offered a middle ground between "feminist empiricism" and "feminist postmodernism," the other major contenders in the usual taxonomy of feminist epistemology. As historian of science Donna Haraway has described:

> Marxist starting points offered tools to get our versions of standpoint theories, insistent embodiment, a rich tradition of critiques of hege-

mony without disempowering positivisms and relativisms, and nuanced theories of mediation. (1991, 186)

Standpoint theory seemed more radical than the "empiricist" approach because it is explicitly political and forthrightly aims to incorporate "women's ways of knowing" that have historically been excluded from science. Yet, it is epistemologically more conservative than the postmodern approach insofar as it does not claim to invalidate the traditional approaches to knowledge, but aims to make them better. Standpoint theory does not deny scientific authority, but hopes to improve it. For this reason, with feminist empiricism, it has been called a project which aims at a "successor science" (Harding 1986).

In the landmark paper, Hartsock wanted to "explore and expand the Marxian argument that socially mediated interaction with nature in the process of production shapes both human beings and theories of knowledge" (1983a, 283). In many ways her argument is classic Marxist feminism. Taking the approach of treating women as a class, she argued that feminists have a position of epistemic privilege. The Marxian picture of the position of the worker as an agent of knowledge is said to even better characterize the position of women:

> The feminist standpoint which emerges through an examination of women's activities is related to the proletarian standpoint, but deeper going. Women and workers inhabit a world in which the emphasis is on change rather than stasis, a world characterized by interaction with natural substances rather than separation from nature, a world in which quality is more important than quantity, a world in which the unification of mind and body is inherent in the activities performed. (Hartsock 1983a, 290)

Women and workers have an enhanced potential for understanding because they are less likely to falsely see themselves in separation from the world. A standpoint, whether that of workers or women, offers more than a *different* perspective; the lack of privilege has *potential advantage* for contributing to knowledge.

More recent standpoint theorists emphasize that the enhanced resources for knowledge arise from the opposition to oppression and not from the experience of oppression. The experience of oppression only forms the foundation, providing the potential for epistemic advantage. Workers and women live life on the social margins: their activities are always directed toward those in power. As such, they are more involved with the social construction of their own positions and the positions of other people, including those in the center. Marginalized people are never wholly out-siders, but "outsiders within," having both to negotiate their own environ-ments, worlds bound by class, gender, race, sexuality, geography, religion, and so forth, and to negotiate the environments of those in the dominant position. Those who are subservient support the lives of those in power and so perpetuate the power structure; they are intimately involved with the mechanisms of social maintenance. Therefore, marginalized people have the potential to see political relationships more clearly than those who simply rely on them, and this potential becomes manifest epistemic advantage when the oppressive conditions are resisted. Focusing on social and political structures can reveal problems and interpretations that are hard to recognize from a central political position. Opposition to oppres-sion provides unique resources for understanding and building knowledge.

ESSENTIALISM IN STANDPOINT THEORY

The "specifically feminist historical materialism" that Hartsock (1983a) proposed and christened "the feminist standpoint" has been re-peatedly charged with essentialism, a problem of great concern for femi-nism since the 1980s. Much of feminism has grossly neglected the variety of women's experiences by treating the observations and problems of Western, white, middle-class, married, heterosexual women as paradig-matic concerns for women. Early standpoint theory is particularly likely to be charged with essentialism, speaking for all women as if women were united by an essence of woman and as if some universal property charac-terized the sexism suffered by different women. Sandra Harding (1986) associated many different and independent approaches together under the rubric of "standpoint theories." The extent to which, and in what manner, they made essentialist claims varied greatly, and in a multitude of ways, they have attempted to resolve this problem. Speaking for women as a whole remains a problem for feminism; however, as I will argue, feminist standpoint theory has developed to eliminate the problematic assumption of uniformity among women. It problematizes the extent to which there are such uniformities, which makes it an indispensable epistemology for feminism.

It is not clear whether, or in what sense, Hartsock is guilty of positing a gender essence to knowledge. Hartsock argues that her Marxist epistemol-ogy avoids attributing a biological essence to the knower:

> the Marxian category of labor, including as it does both interaction
> with other humans and with the natural world can help to cut through

the dichotomy of nature and culture, and for feminists, can help to avoid the false choice of characterizing the situation of women as either "purely natural" or "purely social." (Hartsock 1983a, 289)

Hartsock's equation of the feminine with what is natural gives rise to many of the charges of essentialism. However, this naturalism is partly derived from the Marxian epistemology, which provides an historical context for the material circumstance, thus eliminating essentialist tendencies. Although Hartsock emphasizes the entrenchment of women in nature, complete with reproductive potential, she does not depict this "hyper-natural" femininity as a necessary circumstance.

> [The] facts of motherwork (for some particular cultural group) were called on in some of the original accounts to make the then not so obvious point that women's lives *were and are* different from men's in scientifically and epistemologically significant ways. (Harding 1993, 134)

Because the differences in knowledge that concern standpoint theory are manifestations of oppression, it is implicit that differences result from political circumstances and, therefore, are contingent. These differences are substantial enough to act as dimensions along which knowledge can be analyzed, but this epistemological reification is only for the purpose of change which will subvert the uniformity of the difference.

Hartsock's early association of standpoint theory with the object-relations theory of psychological development encouraged the naturalistic proclivity of Marxist analysis. This psycho-analytic theory supports the premise of standpoint theory that women have different resources for knowledge by explaining how the objects one works with produce different ways of understanding. Object-relations theory explained how women develop different ways of knowing by describing how the objects women work with influence what they learn. Insofar as the objects of women's experience differ from the objects of men's experience, women are said to develop forms of knowledge different from men's. More to the point, women's traditional work is more entrenched in nature, concerned with the specific maintenance of cleaning and feeding and with the support and organization of particular people. On the other hand, men's traditional work is concerned with generalities of culture and only with people at a distance. This entails that knowledge from a women's perspective is more about nature and less about culture. Although object-relations theory can explain how women have unique resources for understanding, locating women closer to nature implies their lesser competence at culture which

might justify limited political activities. Hartsock denies that the entrenchment of women in nature is necessary or essential to their understandings
by describing it as an historical contingency, but it is very difficult to
support the political goal of equality if we accept on any grounds that
"gender locates and limits" women's knowledge (Bordo 1990, 148). Most
importantly, modeling the psychological development of all women on the
experience of white, middle-class, Euro-Americans is unacceptable.

Because Hartsock denies the biological necessity of the association of
women with nature, she is certainly not guilty of biological essentialism
but, instead, of what could be called "material essentialism." That is, she
assumes that women have material circumstances which uniformly differ
from those of men. Material commonalities among women's circumstances provided for "a specifically feminist historical materialism," the
subtitle of the original article. However, to be specifically feminist was not
to be specific enough. Although Hartsock claims to be aware of the danger
of glossing over variations for lesbians and women of colour, this is a bare
acknowledgment of differences among women (1983a, 289-90). More
recently, she recognizes that she originally repeated Marx's mistake.

> By examining the institutional sexual division of labor, I argued that
> a feminist standpoint could be developed that would deepen the
> critique available from the standpoint of the proletariat and that
> would allow for a critique of patriarchal ideology. In following this
> strategy I committed an error similar to that of Marx. While he made
> no theoretical space for any oppression other than class, by follow-
> ing his lead I failed to allow for the importance of differences among
> women and differences among other various groups–power differ-
> ences all. (Hartsock 1997, 368)

Feminism needs to address the variety of women's circumstances and
cannot be modeled on the isolated experiences of relatively privileged
women.

The emerging concern for standpoint theory is how limitations on
knowledge can be counteracted. Material commonalities are now only the
starting point for the development of a standpoint because theories of
psychological development no longer are invoked to explain how resources for knowledge are gendered. Harding's early concerns about
standpoint theory in *The Science Question in Feminism* (1986) affect the
object-relations component more than the Marxist component, as Alison
Wylie (1987, 66-7) argues. The assumption of developmental commonality is much more contentious than the observation of more general commonalities of material experience. Hartsock (1997, 367-8) also notes that

criticisms of standpoint theory have largely neglected the Marxist origins, and Dorothy Smith, who is often credited for her contributions to standpoint theory (cf. 1987), has never wanted anything to do with object-relations theory. Abandoning all claims that psychological development creates different kinds of knowers means that standpoint theory no longer depends on any particular uniform material aspects of women's lives as determinants of women's knowledge. It is no longer assumed that there is one way, or two, or even three, or any definite number of ways in which knowing situations are structured by sexism or any other type of oppression.

Even though Hartsock's assumption of uniform gender experience is troubling, the Marxist depiction of feminist concerns is not essentialist even at a material level because it is a description of a contingency. She must be credited for recognizing the importance of treating the apparent uniformity of women's circumstances *as a problem,* and for recognizing as a resource for knowledge the opposition to those uniform experiences that indicate oppression. The recognition of epistemic benefit from confronting the circumstances of oppression does not originate with Donna Haraway in 1985, as Harding (1986, 192-4) claims, but with Nancy Hartsock in 1983.

> The articulation of a feminist standpoint based on women's relational self-definition and activity exposes the world men have constructed and the self-understanding which manifests these relations as partial and perverse. More importantly, by drawing out the potentiality available in the actuality and thereby exposing the inhumanity of human relations, it embodies a distress which requires a solution. (1983a, 303)

Hartsock argues that the relevance of feminism to knowledge is that it requires a fresh perspective, a "revelation" of a problem that challenges existing political relationships, which thus provides potential for change and new ways of understanding. Oppression itself is not a resource for knowledge; women are advantaged as agents of knowledge only insofar as they oppose sexism and other forms of oppression. Critique and interpretation are needed to exploit the potential for knowledge that is latent in the experience of oppression. Haraway puts it best:

> The standpoints of the subjugated are not 'innocent' positions. On the contrary, they are preferred because in principle they are least likely to allow denial of the critical and interpretative core of all knowledge. (1991, 191)

However, for some even survival is a form of resistance: "self-definition, self-valuation, and movement toward self-reliance inform her world view, beliefs that stem from her struggles to *survive*" (Collins 1990, 140).

As Susan Hekman observes, the late 1980s' turn in standpoint theory moves from the assumption of a common woman's essence to the assumption of difference among women's realities (1997, 349). However, this does not mean that commonality is completely rejected. The concern is how, when there are uniformities, persistent consistent restrictions which any liberatory movement must recognize, the oppressive sameness can be turned to serve liberatory purposes. The commonality must be treated as an artifact. Recognizing commonalities from a standpoint is recognizing contingencies which can be changed.

EMPIRICIST DIMENSIONS OF STANDPOINT THEORY

Although standpoint theory cannot be replaced by empiricism, it must depend on the empiricism inherent in its Marxist origins. The circumstances of the knower in the material world affect the nature of experiences, thus characterizing the nature of a person's empirical resources. Material oppression affects knowledge by affecting the experiences available for building understanding. Some of the best components of recent standpoint theory may seem to be feminist empiricism with problematic rhetoric (Campbell 1994). However, I contest the arguments of Campbell (1994) and Longino (1993) for abandoning standpoint accounts and embracing an empiricism without explicit politics. Standpoint theory improves on feminist empiricism whether we conceive of standpoint epistemology as an enhancement of empiricism or a partner for it.

Empiricism is most evident in Harding's concept of "strong objectivity": the situation of the epistemic agent should be part of the epistemic claim. Harding (1993) argues that knowers should be strongly reflexive: "place the subject of knowledge on the same critical, causal plane as the objects of knowledge" (89). This self-reflexivity emphasizes the historical and material situation of knowers and the impact that this has on capabilities for understanding. Accounting for circumstances enhances understanding by increasing the amount of information about a particular event. As Campbell explains, this epistemic goal can be justified in empiricist terms (1994, 108). Strong reflexivity is accounting for our own situations as knowers: as those who generate models in the context of discovery; and as those who apply models in the context of justification. Describing this situation is an empirical matter and, therefore, what is contributed by strong reflexivity is just increased empirical input.

Longino suggests, and Campbell picks up the point, that standpoint theory must be supported by some form of empiricism.

> It is not clear how any form of standpoint theory that does not endorse something like the empiricist norms of predictive success, observation independence, and explanatory power can explain the worth of testing procedures that seem obviously justified and have been used for worthwhile political ends, say, to refute claims about women's natural inferiority to men. (Campbell 1994, 108)

Feminism requires an empirical foundation against which to evaluate the political generation and interpretation of data. Breadth of experience is a traditional empiricist virtue echoed in many feminist epistemologies, and in this way, the epistemic goals of standpoint theory are the same as those of feminist empiricism. Recent feminist empiricism is particularly concerned with making all dimensions of science politically accountable, requiring that we actively pursue alternative theories because a broader base of considerations enhances awareness and offers an empirical advantage (Longino 1993; Okruhlik 1995). Empiricism has been virtually unacknowledged in standpoint theory, but it is implicit to any success it can have. Sexism, racism, classism, heterosexism, and so forth only can be discovered relative to their empirical foundations or lack of them.

Campbell praises the subversive potential of the explicitly empiricist approach because it requires strong reflexivity without confrontational terminology. He argues that making this requirement within the more accepted empiricist framework has a greater likelihood of success. Empiricist terms are more powerful because they have a better epistemological pedigree than the Marxism of standpoint theory. Moreover, empiricism has no problems accounting for the nature of its feminism, which creates essentialist tendencies in standpoint theory. By not claiming epistemic privilege for any perspective, feminist empiricism encourages all, including feminist, contributions. It need not explain what makes it feminist because it is based only on increasing input to improve understanding. If empiricism can meet feminist needs, it may avoid having to define what it is to be "feminist" and, thereby, avoid the implicit danger of equivocating the variety of women's experiences. Because feminist empiricism embraces a broad variety of contributions and endorses no epistemic privilege, it need not justify why one contribution is accepted over another; this is left to the rigors of contemporary scientific standards. The portrayal of scientific rigors varies according to the theorist. Longino (1993), Campbell (1994), and Kathleen Okruhlik (1995) offer different accounts, but they all rely on some revisioned scientific process.

Longino argues that standpoint theory lacks the prescriptive potential of empiricism because it cannot provide a basis for choosing among standpoints, for locating the perspective that provides advantage for a knower.

> If genuine or better knowledge depends on the correct or a more correct standpoint, social theory is needed to ascertain which of these locations is the epistemologically privileged one. But in a standpoint epistemology, a standpoint is needed to justify such a theory. (1993, 104)

If a standpoint, or a metastandpoint, or a "metanarrative" (Hekman 1997, 355), is necessary to justify the selection of a preferred standpoint, justification seems to fall into an infinite regress. Because standpoint knowledge requires more than the uninterpreted experience of empiricism, it needs some other basis for evaluation. Yet this basis for interpretation must be recognized as appropriate on some further basis if standpoint theory is not reducible to empiricism. We seem to be required to find the best perspective, but the need for an ideal standpoint can never be answered.

MEETING THE EMPIRICIST CHALLENGE

Sandra Harding's original 1986 taxonomy of feminist epistemology, which distinguishes "feminist empiricism" from "standpoint theory," is 10 years old and has increasingly little relevance. Although advocates of standpoint theory remain importantly loyal to the early insights of this approach, Harding herself could quarrel neither with the commonalities that have been observed between it and feminist empiricism nor with the need for it to fall back on some form of empiricism. She has always recognized standpoint epistemology to be in league with feminist empiricism as a "successor science project," aiming to improve science rather than to undermine it (Harding 1986). More recently, she warns against making hasty decisions between the two (Harding 1991, 136-7). Most importantly, although Harding claims to be developing a postmodern standpoint theory, she has also taken some empiricism in tow, as Longino (1993) and Campbell (1994) observe. Harding's formulation of standpoint epistemology is perfectly compatible with empiricism and even depends on empiricism. Although Harding does not explore the potential for this alliance, other recent work on standpoint theory, especially that of Patricia Hill Collins (1990), shows great potential for an account that has enough commonality with feminist empiricism to work in tandem with it but which goes beyond empiricism in fruitful ways. Standpoint theory is distinguished from the tradition of feminist empiricism by telling us *where* to look for alternative hypotheses not just that we should pursue them. The pure empiricist prescription to pursue different perspectives is outstripped by the direction to generate hypotheses that challenge oppression. This counters Longino's (1993) charge that standpoint epistemology lacks normative capacity, offering no prescription for action: oppositional consciousness blocks the potential for regress in developing a standpoint. It also shows why the confrontational character of standpoint theory is necessary, contra Campbell (1994), for enhancing empiricist resources in a way that will accommodate feminist concerns.

The epistemic advantage of self-reflexivity has empirical content, as Campbell (1994) argues, but this content is achieved by political means: a knower must achieve oppositional consciousness to acquire a standpoint, thus increasing the range of experience available. Standpoint theory advocates looking to marginal experience for fresh information. That is much like feminist empiricism; but standpoint theory also argues that these valuable insights can be achieved only by resistance to the conditions of marginalization. The articulation which distinguishes standpoints from each other and from the mainstream, and which can enhance understanding, is not something that is found but is created. In order to get the unique resources for knowledge which standpoint theorists argue can be found, for example, in black feminism, one must engage in the projects of black feminism; one must oppose the situation that created the condition in which the standpoint could emerge and create a new situation. A standpoint is not just a political body or a social category, but it must be self-consciously political in terms of country, race, sexuality, and religion. Each standpoint characterizes oppression differently because the understanding arises out of a different type of experience of oppression. The oppression of blacks is not the same as that of lesbians or of the rural poor, and each must be allowed to articulate itself as an experienced commonality and common injustice. (Regarding those in the center who claim to be oppressed, such as men's groups, white supremacists, and the "religious right," input will be redundant where claims of oppression are not true. They will be weeded out by the empiricist virtue of maximizing input breadth.)

Contemporary standpoint theory emphasizes the need for political opposition to bring out the potential for increasing knowledge that is latent in the experience of oppression. Although some early standpoint theorists avoided pretensions to the universal representation of women by speaking from specific positions, they sometimes took the experience of oppression from that perspective to be an epistemic resource. This essentializes the experience of oppression: even if we are speaking only of black women or only of lesbians, the experience of oppression is not uniform. To work around the problem of essentialism, current theory focuses on the need for political opposition to bring out the potential for epistemic advantage. It only is latent in the perspective of the oppressed, and it is very difficult to make manifest:

> to see from below is neither easily learned nor unproblematic, even if 'we' 'naturally' inhabit the great underground terrain of subjugated knowledges. (Haraway 1991, 191)

Standpoint theory advises looking for alternative hypotheses through political engagement whether it is based on one's own experience of oppression or based on engaging the problems faced by others. The original Marxian materialism limits who is capable of achieving knowledge from a certain standpoint such that those at the center cannot learn from standpoints. Hartsock describes:

> there are some perspectives on society from which, however well intentioned one may be, the real relations of humans with each other and with the natural world are not visible. (Hartsock 1983b, 117)

However, this restriction is not accepted by feminist standpoint theorists, whose approach is "Marxism," which is only *derived* from the original "Marxian" analysis and need not be bound by its determinism. Essentialist tendencies are counteracted by "thinking from the perspective of other others," in Harding's terms (1991, 180-1), and "resistance to the matrix of domination" (Collins 1990, 229-30). When we are able to oppose oppression, the circumstances it creates can reveal information that is hidden from within a position of power.

   Longino's arguments against standpoint theory are based on its privileging the position of an individual knower. However, standpoint theory is not an individualistic epistemology in the problematic way she describes. What facilitates the achievement of standpoint knowledge and eliminates the potential for infinite regress in determining a standpoint is that standpoint knowledge is built out of the particular experiences of individuals by interaction of people and of groups with each other. Longino suggests

> that scientific knowledge is constructed not by individuals applying a method to the material to be known but by individuals in interaction with one another in ways that modify their observations, theories and hypotheses, and patterns of reasoning. (1993, 111)

Collins makes similar considerations by asserting the importance of the rearticulation of experience to a standpoint. The collected various experiences of black women that become considered as a common experience of oppression when articulated by black feminists are thereby transformed into a collective experience and consciousness. Collins' argument that standpoints can only be developed through their contrast with one another and with dominant views is akin to Longino's view that "scientific knowledge . . . is an outcome of the critical dialogue in which individuals and groups holding different points of view engage with each other" (1993, 112). Recently, commenting on Hekman in *Signs*, Collins has reiterated the centrality of groups to standpoint theory.

> The notion of standpoint refers to groups having shared histories based on their shared location in relations of power–standpoints arise neither from crowds of individuals nor from groups analytically created by scholars and bureaucrats. (Collins 1997, 376)

Collins, more than any of the others who align themselves with standpoint theory, has recognized the crucial role of community to standpoints. However, she is not alone. Witness recent Hartsock: "to claim that we can understand the totality of social relations from a single perspective is as futile an effort as to claim that we can see everything from nowhere" (1997, 371). Although some views are better than others, no view is complete. Achieving a standpoint is not finding the right, ideal perspective but opposing the political limitations on perspectives. No metastandpoint is required, just the politically purposeful concerted interactions of individuals. The interaction of people with different experiences within a perspective is necessary for developing a standpoint. As Catherine M. O'Leary argues in this volume, the standpoint theories developed by black feminists, Collins and bell hooks, benefit from treating collective identity not as fragmentation from the larger collective but as built up from the particular experiences of individuals. However, the standpoint does not arise until group identity is recognized as a point of resistance.

Although each is uniquely based on the collaboration of individuals, standpoints are not isolated. Developing a standpoint requires learning from other independently articulated perspectives.

> The significance of seeing race, class, and gender as interlocking systems of oppression is that such an approach fosters a paradigmatic shift of thinking inclusively about other oppressions, such as age, sexual orientation, religion, and ethnicity . . . Other people of colour, Jews, the poor, white women, and gays and lesbians have all had

similar ideological justifications offered for their subordination. (Collins 1990, 225)

In all cases, the self-definition of a standpoint requires both coalition with and differentiation from other groups. Collins (1990) argues that intellectuals are vital to the development of standpoints because they facilitate self-definition by a group (35-37). Intellectuals provide all parties with greater access to information. Black feminist intellectuals provide an intellectual resource both for other intellectuals and for other black women.

The importance of the interplay of various social groups to the development of a standpoint is also evident, if not so explicit, in Harding's *Whose Science? Whose Knowledge?* (1991, 14, 70-71, 282). Standpoint knowledge must be achievable by embracing another's struggle. For example, not all and only women, or all and only women from a particular location, can achieve a feminist standpoint. What is required is for men to contribute to feminism and white women to contribute to black feminism, and how such contributions can be possible in a standpoint theory are open questions. However, such possibilities and such histories of contribution must be recognized. Because of the dependence of standpoints on the interactions of different groups of people, those who do not share a certain form of material oppression may contribute to the development of a standpoint from that oppressed circumstance.

There is no predetermined preferential position; the importance of any perspective is its ability to challenge traditional contexts for understanding a particular situation. Strong objectivity requires that we focus on attendant oppression, *self*-reflexivity. We can best add to our understandings by finding out how someone opposing a less-privileged perspective on the same situation would understand what we are observing. Harding describes how her own recent work generates new resources for understanding science:

> Postcolonial science studies . . . provide resources that northern and northern feminist science studies cannot provide . . . because thought that begins from conceptual framework developed to answer questions arising in *their* lives starts from outside the Eurocentric conceptual frameworks within which northern and northern feminist science studies have been largely organized. (1997, 385)

The only general background condition for recognizing the potential for a standpoint and for achieving standpoint knowledge is opposition to oppression. Oppression may be opposed in whatever way it can to shed light on a particular event. Achieving a standpoint is a matter of applying a political disposition. It is not priorly determinable by a calculus but is established by resistance to whatever political limitations may be attendant. Chela Sandoval (1991) has argued that United States-Third World feminists are particularly able to navigate a variety of epistemic environments. Although she sees oppositional consciousness as a step in developing feminist consciousness that goes beyond standpoint theory, it can be viewed as an aspect of standpoint theory. In the same way that traversing class boundaries is supposed to provide workers with better knowledge in Marxist epistemology, and traversing gender boundaries is supposed to provide access to greater epistemic resources for feminists, United States-Third world women have even greater potential for epistemic advantage. Sandoval (1991) argues that moving among different epistemic perspectives aids in the development of political self-consciousness in one's home epistemic environment (1991). I add only that where political self-consciousness involves resistance to oppression a standpoint is developed.

Against Campbell's protest that essentialism continues to mar standpoint theory, I propose that the virtue of standpoint theory is that it targets the uniformity created by oppression. Any gendered aspects of knowledge that standpoint theory addresses are not blithely assumed, as if they were essential, but directly confronted and problematized, thereby recognized as contingent. A standpoint is created through opposition to the circumstances of oppression. The experiences of individuals must be rearticulated to reflect their coherence as a type of experience of oppression (Collins 1990, 30-33). What this entails is seizing the socially structured commonality, the particular form of oppression, and reshaping it to suit the purposes of the oppressed. Examples of this include the reappropriation of language, such as "dyke" by lesbians, and even the development of feminist epistemologies themselves. The production of a standpoint in order to achieve politicized knowledge requires attention to the factors which constructed that particular epistemic environment as an unpoliticized perspective. The provisional assumption of standpoint theory is that a knower's situation is affected by dimensions of oppression, such as race, class, sexuality, and sex. However, observed uniformities in limitations along the axes of oppression are not accepted but identified so that they may be resisted. Standpoint epistemology redresses what is common among the various personal experiences of oppression; it encourages emancipatory understandings by recognizing the individual experience as part of a social pattern. Although Dorothy Smith (1997) has no interest in developing an epistemology for feminism, her account of how women's perspectives are developed shows how political momentum is created by addressing the commonalities of women's experience.

> When we assembled *as* "women" and spoke together *as* "women," constituting "women" as a category of political mobilization, we discovered dimensions of "our" experience that had no prior discursive definition. (394)

What is common varies among different oppressions, but by addressing common problems, the social underpinnings of personal trials can be assessed.

Standpoints take advantage of the dynamic nature of the social aspects of knowledge. Nancy J. Hirschmann argues in this volume that the static nature of a standpoint is only provisional; the material content of a standpoint is only a fleeting "moment" in history. I concur that the perspective out of which a standpoint is developed must be fundamentally conceived as transitional. This is the crucial point of nexus in a standpoint between the descriptive material world and the prescriptive political world. As Smith (1997) argues, the social aspects of knowledge are not static. "The social is always *being brought into being* in the concerting of people's local activities. It is never already there" (395). The commonality created in a standpoint from diverse experiences acts as a focus of resistance for liberatory epistemology. I emphasize that this movement from description to prescription makes standpoint theory action-oriented. Knowers can take charge of the social dynamic, recognizing the possibility to "select, engage, and disengage gears in a system for the transmission of power" (Sandoval 1991, 14). Taking advantage of this potential for directing knowledge allows knowers to change the circumstances that produce oppression. Once we have reclaimed "the master's tools," then can we "dismantle the master's house." This is not to say that the meanings of social practices can be turned on their heads at will. It is to suggest that essentializing aspects of culture are actively thwarted by commonplace feminist practice in a manner that standpoint theory explains, encourages, and justifies as a contribution to human knowledge. By taking charge of their epistemic environments and confronting the political circumstances that limit knowledge, people can increase their resources for understanding.

Insofar as feminist empiricism does not recognize oppression as an epistemic influence, it fails to address how perspectives which can enhance empirical resources may be hidden. If we are to follow the empiricist aim of encouraging diverse input to science, we must account for the way oppression limits empirical resources. The oppressed are debilitated materially and, therefore, epistemically. A person's ability to understand is affected by their environment and particularly limited when that environment has been exceptionally limited, as under oppression. Oppression restricts experience and education, therefore, it restricts the gaining and the sharing of understanding. Longino (1993, 118) admits that her approach risks discounting politically marginalized approaches. Views from the margin are likely to have trouble reaching the public forum of science, and empiricism cannot in itself redress this problem. Standpoint epistemology directs the knower to consider as part of knowledge claims whether oppression might affect the type of understanding that is available and to compensate for any influence of oppression by attending to the perspective of those resisting the attendant oppression.

Standpoint theory is a more pointedly political epistemology than feminist empiricism. For this reason, it is also more pointedly feminist. Achieving standpoint knowledge requires people to consider specifically the epistemic import of the conditions which made feminism and other liberatory movements necessary. In accounting for the influence of power differentials on our knowledge claims, we work to counteract the epistemic roadblocks that prevent politically marginalized perspectives from being articulated and from being heard. For feminist empiricism, standpoint theory presents an alternative to the traditional standards for assessing the validity of particular perspectives. Unless we can include opposition to oppression as a resource in these traditions, we will lose valuable empirical resources. The empiricist approach allows the results of feminist research to seem more plausible, and "once they are considered plausible, the feminist claims wreak havoc within networks of traditional belief" (Harding 1991, 113). The rhetoric and vision of feminist empiricism imply that feminism can be assimilated to science, but if it does not distinguish emancipatory perspectives as deserving greater attention, then it fails to meet its own goals of maximizing experiential input. Empirical resources cannot be plucked from the oppressed; these resources for knowledge must be nurtured by opposing the circumstances that make them marginal.

WHERE STANDPOINT STANDS NOW

The idea that oppositional consciousness offers epistemic advantage originates with Hartsock's attempt to formulate a standpoint not of women but of feminists. In the long run, therefore, she is not guilty of material essentialism but must be credited for problematizing the extent to which those who are oppressed share debilitating material circumstances. These circumstances can prevent the articulation of views from the margin; and standpoint theory continues to be distinguished by redressing these impediments to broad empirical input. Although the direct grappling with categories of oppression has brought charges of essentialism against the theory, at the core of its radical potential is its ability to turn oppressive categories into tools for liberation. Although standpoint theory can gain philosophical and practical credibility through alignment with feminist empiricism, the oppositional consciousness of a standpoint offers the key ingredient for a prescription that will undermine the conservative tendencies in science. Feminist empiricism risks neglecting valuable and unique epistemic resources insofar as it does not facilitate the production of perspectives from the political margin.

As do other feminist epistemologies, standpoint theory predicts its own demise, yet there is reason to believe that time has not come. Recent feminist empiricism has embraced its own contingency as a type of knowledge of the contingency of knowledge (Nelson 1993). Standpoint theory with its Marxist origins is similarly disposed to self-effacing historicism: we must consider ourselves as agents of knowledge and as theorists of knowledge on the same historical material plane as the objects of our knowledge. Standpoint epistemology grew out of the conditions of marginalization of workers and of women. New theories must be expected to arise and supersede it out of other historical contingencies. However, the tools of a standpoint are still very valuable for creating knowledge. What makes standpoint theory an important epistemology for feminism is that it rushes its own demise by addressing the epistemic significance of oppression. It challenges the specific circumstances that give rise to standpoints and to standpoint theories which go unrecognized on a more strictly empiricist account.

REFERENCES

Susan Bordo. 1990. "Feminism, Postmodernism, and Gender-Scepticism." In *Feminism/Postmodernism,* ed. Linda J. Nicholson. New York: Routledge.
Campbell, Richmond. 1994. "The Virtues of Feminist Empiricism." *Hypatia* 9(1): 90-115.
Collins, Patricia Hill. 1990. *Black Feminist Thought.* Boston: Unwin Hyman.
Collins, Patricia Hill. 1997. "Comments on Hekman's 'Truth and Method: Feminist Standpoint Theory Revisited': Where's the Power?" *Signs* 22(2):375-381.
Haraway, Donna. 1991. "Situated Knowledges: The Science Question in Feminism and the Privilege of Partial Perspective." In *Simians, Cyborgs, Women: The Reinvention of Nature.* New York: Routledge.
Harding, Sandra. 1986. *The Science Question in Feminism.* Ithaca: Cornell University Press.
_____. 1991. *Whose Science? Whose Knowledge?* Ithaca: Cornell University Press.

_____. 1993. "Rethinking Standpoint Epistemology: 'What is Strong Objectivity?'" In *Feminist Epistemologies,* ed. Linda Alcoff and Elizabeth Potter. New York: Routledge.

Hartsock, Nancy C. M. 1983a. "The Feminist Standpoint: Towards a Specifically Feminist Historical Materialism." In *Discovering Reality,* ed. Sandra Harding and Merrill Hintikka. Dordrecht: D. Reidel.

_____. 1983b. *Money, Sex and Power.* New York: Longman.

_____. 1997. "Comment on Hekman's 'Truth and Method: Feminist Standpoint Theory Revisited.'" *Signs* 22: 367-374.

Hekman, Susan. 1997. "Truth and Method: Feminist Standpoint Theory Revisited." *Signs* 22: 341-365.

Longino, Helen E. 1993. "Subjects, Power and Knowledge: Description and Prescription in Feminist Philosophies of Science." In *Feminist Epistemologies,* ed. Linda Alcoff and Elizabeth Potter. New York: Routledge.

Nelson, Lynn Hankinson. 1993. "Epistemological Communities." In *Feminist Epistemologies,* ed. Linda Alcoff and Elizabeth Potter. New York: Routledge.

Okruhlik, Kathleen. 1995. "Gender and the Biological Sciences." *Canadian Journal of Philosophy* supplementary volume 20: 21-42.

Sandoval, Chela. 1991. "U.S. Third World Feminism: The Theory and Method of Oppositional Consciousness in the Postmodern World." *Genders* 10: 2-24.

Smith, Dorothy E. 1997. "Comment on Hekman's 'Truth and Method: Feminist Standpoint Theory Revisited.'" *Signs* 22: 392-398.

_____. 1987. "Women's Perspective as a Radical Critique of Sociology." In *Feminism and Methodology,* ed. Sandra Harding. Bloomington: Indiana University Press.

Wylie, Alison. 1987. "The Philosophy of Ambivalence: Sandra Harding on 'The Science Question in Feminism.'" *Canadian Journal of Philosophy,* supplementary volume 13: 59- 85.

Counteridentification
or Counterhegemony?
Transforming Feminist Standpoint Theory

Catherine M. O'Leary

SUMMARY. In this paper I develop a theoretical approach that reha-
bilitates identity as a political and interpretive, not essentialist, category. To this end, I explore versions of feminist standpoint theory developed by Nancy Hartsock and Alison Jaggar. While these versions of
standpoint theory have marked the significance of experience and
knowledge for feminist practice, their conception of subjectivity is too
unified and, therefore, creates problems for addressing the epistemological implications of "difference." For this approach to feminist
subjectivity, power relations of race, class, and nation are "differences" which are viewed as threatening endless fragmentation or
promising plurality. Alternatively, following Norma Alarcón's theory
of multiple-voiced subjectivity, I argue that relations of power produce complex subjectivities situated within multiple, intersecting axes
of power: race, class, sex, gender, nation. These relations of power
mark the terrain of experience as an interpretive field for the production of knowledge and collective identity. This approach shifts the
interpretation of experience and knowledge from a paradigm of essen-

I would like to thank Kamala Visweswaran for her intellectual guidance and
encouragement, and for very helpful readings: Ira Katznelson, Marion Smiley,
Jane Mansbridge, Victoria Hattam, Orville Lee, and Piya Chatterjee. These
thanks, of course, do not necessarily reflect agreement with my argument, and any
remaining shortcomings are my responsibility.

An earlier version of this project was presented at the Annual Meeting of the
American Political Science Association, September 1994.

[Haworth co-indexing entry note]: "Counteridentification or Counterhegemony? Transforming
Feminist Standpoint Theory." O'Leary, Catherine M. Co-published simultaneously in *Women & Politics* (The Haworth Press, Inc.) Vol. 18, No. 3, 1997, pp. 45-72; and: *Politics and Feminist Standpoint
Theories* (ed: Sally J. Kenney and Helen Kinsella) The Haworth Press, Inc., 1997, pp. 45-72. Single or
multiple copies of this article are available for a fee from The Haworth Document Delivery Service
[1-800-342-9678, 9:00 a.m. - 5:00 p.m. (EST). E-mail address: getinfo@haworth.com].

tialism, fragmentation, and pluralist difference to a paradigm of accountability and coalition. *[Article copies available for a fee from The Haworth Document Delivery Service: 1-800-342-9678. E-mail address: getinfo@haworth.com]*

FEMINIST THEORY: IDENTITY, KNOWLEDGE, AND POWER

Living as we did–on the edge–we developed a particular way of seeing reality. We looked both from the outside in and from the inside out. We focused our attention on the center as well as the margin . . . This sense of wholeness, impressed upon our consciousness by the structure of our daily lives, provided us an oppositional world view–a mode of seeing unknown to most of our oppressors, that sustained us, aided us in our struggle to transcend poverty and despair, strengthened our sense of self and our solidarity. (hooks 1984, ix)

This passage from bell hooks' *Feminist Theory: From Margin to Center* places the relationship between knowledge, identity, and politics squarely on the table of contemporary feminist theory. This is certainly not a new issue in political theory, but it has gained renewed relevance given current conflicts and debates over the status of "identity" for establishing the authority to advance political claims. The conceptualization of this category of identity provides a point of entry into central theoretical and political controversies of the past 30 years between structuralists and poststructuralists, between allies of the Subject and its critics (Nicholson 1990). These theoretical disputes have taken on a particularly heated political significance as they have entered the domain of feminist theory, analysis, and practice because debates about the character of subjectivity and consciousness call into question not only the basis, but even the possibility, of traditional forms of political solidarity and collectivity (Barrett and Phillips 1992). Thus feminist theorists, marked as they are by an awareness of and, I hope, a commitment to, a political bottom line in theoretical practice, have been particularly concerned to assess the implications that critiques of Enlightenment conceptions of rationality, subjectivity, and consciousness have for forms of feminist praxis. The positioning of feminist theorists vis-à-vis critical, political practices creates the possibility for a productive and challenging recognition of, and hence accountability for, the effects of power present in the representational and discursive practices that are central to the production of feminist knowledge. This is the metatheoretical punchline to my more specific theoretical argument which analyzes the conception of and relationship between experience, knowledge and identity in feminist standpoint theories.

"Postmodern" critiques of subjectivity, transcendent reason, and the meta-narratives of historical progress have been alternately welcomed, tolerated, feared, and rejected by contemporary feminist theorists (Benhabib et al. 1995). In works which set out to explore the implications of such postmodern critiques for feminist theorizing, the deconstructionist critique of essentialism and the attendant critiques of modern conceptions of subjectivity and rationality are explored for their usefulness in theorizing not only gender difference, but also differences among women (Nicholson 1990; Barrett and Phillips 1992). In response to such theoretical moves, Seyla Benhabib claims that postmodernists, in exalting the multiplicity of difference and performativity of identity, jeopardize the epistemological and normative foundations of an emancipatory feminist theory and practice (Benhabib 1995). Instead, she argues for the "ability to take the 'standpoints of others' and to reverse perspectives in moral reasoning" (Benhabib 1992, 145-46). In "Feminist Encounters: Locating the Politics of Experience," Chandra Mohanty (1992) challenges both a narrow "identity politics," rooted in a pluralist celebration of differences, as well as universalist gender politics which seek to transcend such power hierarchies as race and class, read as mere differences, which fracture the category "woman." By Mohanty's reading, the differences which divide and distinguish women's political experiences can be reduced *neither* to pluralist multiplicity *nor* to transcendent gender commonality. In exploring the category of experience itself, by means of theorizing the operations of racial, national, and class power, Mohanty (1992) argues for the political character of experience as a site for engagement, struggle, and conflict (74-77).[1]

Mohanty's analysis of experience avoids a naive empiricism which would view personal experience as a self-authenticating claim to knowledge and political opinion. Such interpretations of knowledge and experience have prompted the skepticism of postmodern critics who worry that epistemology as a project is implicated in an essentialist conception of the rational subject.[2] But Mohanty's analysis refigures experience as a political category, rooted not in purely psychological phenomena, but in the discursive and material structures of power that inform political practice. I seek to extend this analysis of experience to the categories of knowledge and identity and to explore the possible treatment of each category as well as their interrelationships. By doing so, I seek to develop the theoretical means of rehabilitating identity as a political and interpretive, not essentialist, category.[3]

The theoretical exploration of experience, knowledge, and identity has been a central analytic concern of feminist standpoint theory. Thus, in this discussion of political identity I will focus on the central arguments of feminist standpoint theory, on critical responses to the universalist dimension of such standpoint theory, and on versions of standpoint theory which propose to refigure the treatment of difference and identity. Feminist standpoint theories generally hold that because knowledge is socially constructed, one's position in society informs one's understanding of that society. Furthermore, and more contestedly, as structures of domination and exploitation are central to the dynamics of any society, those who experience forms of oppression will best understand those structures of domination and, thus, certain central dynamics of their society. This interpretation of knowledge has taken various and contested forms within feminist theory. For example, Nancy Hartsock has produced one version which argues for the existence of a universal feminist standpoint; Patricia Hill Collins has developed a version which centers on Black women's standpoint.[4]

I will argue that while feminist standpoint theory has been responsible for marking and analyzing the significance of experience, knowledge, and identity for feminist theory, the universalist version of standpoint theory is problematic in its conception of gender and difference at an *epistemological* level. Much has been written about how feminist standpoint theories deny differences among and power between women. Hartsock, a key standpoint theorist, has acknowledged that her earlier formulations of feminist standpoint "failed to allow for the importance of differences among women and differences among other various groups–power differences all" (1997, 368). But, I will argue these differences continue to be conceived of sociologically, while the epistemological implications of race, class, sex, and nation for standpoint theory are still not broadly recognized. For example, Susan Hekman's (1997) recent paper, which is devoted to the question of epistemology and standpoint theory, persists in treating "difference" at the sociological level. Her resulting solution to the "problem" of multiplicity for standpoint theory is Weber's ideal type, which provides a mechanism for acknowledging plurality at the empirical level, while preserving a formal analytical standpoint for the production of knowledge. For Hekman, "difference" remains separate from, because it is a problem for, the production of knowledge. Instead, I seek to bring issues of power, the forms of power which produce differences of race, class, gender, nation, and sex, to the center of an analysis of standpoint knowledge. I will argue that forms of standpoint theory, such as those developed by Patricia Hill Collins and bell hooks which propose to refigure the status of knowledge and identity for political practice by employing experience as a political and interpretive category, represent alternatives which transform feminist standpoint theory in promising and empowering ways. These theorists grapple with the implications of race for the epistemological, not sociological, analysis of difference and power in feminist theory.

Thus, my own argument draws upon the arguments of others, but also, I believe, upon their standpoints. I, a bourgeois white woman, open this essay with hooks's analysis of growing up a black child in the South. *Her words* cut to the heart of what this paper is about: the potentially transformative quality of certain standpoints and their theorization. *My use* of her words also touches upon what this paper is about: experience is inscribed fundamentally in power relations and seeking to understand experiences of social domination, racism, sexism, heterosexism, class exploitation, colonialism, from a position of political privilege will always risk and perhaps will always involve to some extent one particular articulation of hegemony, appropriation. But *my writing* of this paper is also itself what this paper is about: the urgent political need to grapple with and clarify the counterhegemonic potential of experience, knowledge, and identity in the face of the intransigent dominations of race, gender, sex, nation, class, body: those multi-valent systems of discursive and material practice which structure society, empower, and dominate in complex and contradictory ways. As I move through discussions of these authors' texts and arguments, I am not seeking to provide a review of the contributions to feminist standpoint theory. Instead, this is a strategic theoretical reading of a series of texts: strategic in the sense that the selection of the texts enables specific theoretical interrogations by myself but also, differently perhaps, by the reader. Thus, my writing strategy attempts to grapple with the question of accountability by opening the question of appropriation and then acting within that question.

This paper has four parts. First, I will discuss Nancy Hartsock's and Alison Jaggar's versions of feminist standpoint theory.[5] I have selected key texts by these authors because they exemplify central issues for standpoint theory as a theoretical and political project. My purpose is not to offer a comprehensive assessment of these authors' bodies of work (or that of the other authors I discuss, for that matter) but to examine the implications of particular theoretical strategies for developing feminist standpoint theory. As such, by drawing upon Chandra Mohanty's distinction between transcendence and engagement, I will argue that Hartsock and Jaggar develop, within the bounds of their own theories, a politics of transcendence (1992, 83, 86). However, I will also argue that beyond the immediate bounds of their theories which are threatened by the failure of a transcendental gender project, their conception of epistemology and practice produce a logic of fragmentation that is incapable of mediation. Next, I will consider Norma Alarcón's and Donna Haraway's criticisms of standpoint theory. Although, contrary to the feminist standpoint theorists, both Alarcón and Haraway are developing a politics of "engagement." They pursue such engaged and situated politics in different ways: Haraway by focusing on the concept of objectivity, and Alarcón by focusing on the concept of "multiple-voiced subjectivity." Third, I will address Patricia Hill Collins's and bell hooks' versions of standpoint theory, arguing that they break out of the stance of "counteridentification" which Alarcón rejects and refigure standpoint theory as a transforming and subversive expression of subjectivities and community (Alarcón 1990, 358). Although Collins and hooks would not completely satisfy Alarcón's objections to a theory of "unified subjectivity," in politically significant ways they are endeavoring to claim such "unified subjectivity" for their communities (Alarcón 1990, 364). By addressing the works of Collins and hooks, my purpose is to examine how their different theoretical treatments of experience help to establish the primacy of experience (as an interpretive category) in refiguring standpoint theory and thereby serve to displace the primacy of identity which has marked the forms of standpoint theory I discuss initially. Finally, in the light of this discussion of standpoint theories, I briefly consider Bernice Johnson Reagon's, Gloria Anzaldúa's, and Chandra Mohanty's efforts to refigure the status of experience, knowledge, and identity in politics through the concept of coalition.

The concepts of a politics of engagement and coalition provided by Mohanty and Reagon offer an answer to both poststructuralist anxiety about the power of identity claims and the anxiety of some feminists about the multiplicity of difference. Claims to knowledge and identity *are* forms of power. To put it simply: that is the point. And *exactly because* the mobilization of knowledge rooted in interpretations of experience *is* so powerful, such claims must be clarified as inherently political interpretations (not essential, authentic truths). As such, these claims can be legitimately open to questions of accountability on a range of grounds. The requirement for accountability spurs a process of discovery of multiple and variegated forms of domination, as new language is developed to analyze and name forms of power which operate to subjugate and/or liberate. Hand in hand with the development of these new languages, the innovation of alternative strategies of mobilization that are emancipatory and counterhegemonic becomes possible. By reformulating the question of difference (yea or nay?) as a question of power (in what form?), femi-

nist standpoint theory can move beyond both essentialism and fragmentation to a politics of coalition and accountability.[6] This, by my reading, is
the possible promise of transforming feminist standpoint theory.

WOMEN'S STANDPOINT THEORY: UNIVERSALIZING GENDER

In *Feminist Politics and Human Nature,* Alison Jaggar (1983) describes
four forms of feminism: liberal, Marxist, radical, and socialist. Locating
the most complete articulation of women's standpoint theory in socialist
feminism, Jaggar also identifies variations of standpoint logic in both
feminist and traditional versions of liberal and Marxist theories as well as
in radical feminist thought. Jaggar's analytic approach helps to clarify the
centrality of a standpoint logic in this diverse range of theories and, thereby, helps to lay the conceptual groundwork for the analysis of feminist
standpoint theory.

Predicated upon the principle of value-neutrality in both its positive-
scientific and normative forms, archetypal liberal theorists are preoccupied with specifying rules to order the production of knowledge. Such
rules are seen to eliminate bias caused by particular values or interests
(Jaggar 1983, 356). According to this view, by adopting a detached standpoint achieved by rigorous adherence to established methodology, the
positivist scientist produces value-neutral knowledge. Normative liberal
theory seeks to achieve a similar neutrality in deriving its normative
claims. John Rawls' original position, which exists behind the "veil of
ignorance," uses an explicit standpoint metaphor to describe the location
from which, ignorant of their positions in society and thus impartial,
"rational" people would agree to the fair and unbiased rules which should
order society (cited in Jaggar 1983, 357). Liberal feminists, such as Susan
Moller Okin, who operate within these metatheoretical liberal parameters,
focus criticism on particular gendered assumptions and implications of
reasoning in Rawls' original position. Okin is concerned about the implications of male-female gender difference and the existence of a gender
hierarchy for a universalist theory of justice. She argues that the Rawlsian
project of justice makes theoretically significant assumptions about the
"division of labor between the sexes" and criticizes the "effects that
assumptions about the gendered structure of society have had on thinking
about social justice" (Okin 1989, 230-31, 229). Seeking to rehabilitate the
Rawlsian original position through a "feminist approach to social justice,"
Okin argues that the theoretical distinction between an ethic of justice and
an ethic of care is rooted in inaccurate "gendered" assumptions and that,
contrary to these assumptions, an ethic of care is compatible with an ethic

of justice (229-230, 246). Okin's liberal feminism is concerned to overcome gender difference in order to secure the impartial, universalist standpoint which provides the foundation for her theory of justice.[7] This brief
consideration of how standpoint operates in liberal theory is relevant to the
analysis of feminist standpoint theory not only as a clarifying contrast, but
as an indication of connections. While Hartsock and Jaggar reject the
presumed neutrality of the liberal standpoint, their own version of standpoint theory shares a similar universalism. And while Haraway's (1988)
critique of standpoint theory calls for partial knowledges, she seeks to
retain a concept of objectivity.

In contrast to liberal feminist theory, Marxist social theory and epistemology are critical for both Jaggar's and Hartsock's accounts of standpoint theory (Hartsock 1983, 117, 231; Jaggar 1983, 125). Rejecting the
scientific claims of certain strains of Marxism, Jaggar and Hartsock favor
Lukács's sociology of knowledge which denies the possibility of a neutral,
detached epistemological stance. Lukács (1971) argues that all knowledge
is a product of social activity and, thus, is shaped by the interests and
concerns of its creators. "Consequently, no knowledge can be objective in
the liberal or positive sense" (Jaggar 1983, 362).[8] Thus, according to this
reading, "standpoint" is central for the production and interpretation of
knowledge claims. "Different social positions provide different vantage
points from which some aspects of reality come into prominence and from
which other aspects are obscured" (Jaggar 1983, 361). Jaggar also adopts
Lukács's criterion for evaluating knowledge and consciousness which
prioritizes the standpoint of those who benefit least from the existing
social structure because they will be most inclined to produce knowledge
that demystifies the existing social order (Jaggar 1983, 362).[9] Although
Jaggar criticizes Marxist feminism for its inability "to conceive that
women might have their own epistemological standpoint," the Marxist
concept of standpoint is foundational for her own women's standpoint
theory (Jaggar 1983, 363). Thus, it is important to note that this foundational formulation of standpoint theory, which claims that knowledge is
subjective in the sense that it is rooted in a particular subject position
(bourgeois or proletarian), conceives of those subject positions as objective, as a necessary consequence of the mode of production. This interpretation provides Marxist theory itself with a meta-level objective standpoint, creating the gap, from the standpoint of the theorist, between theory
and practice, the "problem" of false consciousness. This phenomenon
reappears, in a somewhat different form, in feminist standpoint theory.

Building on her analysis of Marxist conceptions of standpoint, Jaggar
credits radical feminism with putting the "woman" in women's standpoint

theory. Expounding upon women's forms of knowledge, "the radical feminist critique of patriarchal modes of knowing recalls traditional Marxist critiques of the liberal/positivist paradigm of knowledge" (Jaggar 1983, 364-65). Radical feminism emphasizes the universal quality of women's standpoint, a standpoint characterized by prioritizing feelings and immediate experience, holding a relational, interconnected worldview, and using emotionally evocative and often non-linear forms of expression to "demystify myths through which [men's] domination [of women] is concealed" (Jaggar 1983, 369). While acknowledging the contribution of radical feminism's woman-centered approach, Jaggar is skeptical of its emotive and experiential form. "[T]he standpoint of women is not expressed directly in women's naive and unreflective world view" (Jaggar 1983, 371).

Jaggar and Hartsock offer very similar syntheses of Marxism's standpoint analysis and radical feminism's woman-centered approach. Starting from the premise that "the special social or class position of women gives them a special epistemological standpoint which makes possible a view of the world that is more reliable and less distorted than that available either to capitalist or to working-class men," Jaggar proceeds to discuss those forms of knowledge which are available from women's standpoint. Women's role in history, distinctive psychological and moral development, and forms of labor, all largely ignored or discounted by patriarchal forms of knowledge, are brought to light by this form of analysis (Jaggar 1983, 372-74). Hartsock particularly emphasizes the sexual division of labor as a starting point for "the construction of a feminist standpoint on which to ground a specifically feminist historical materialism" (Hartsock 1983, 231). Hartsock uses the term "feminist" standpoint to underscore that such a standpoint is not immediately available to women but must be achieved (1983, 232). As women's role in the sexual division of labor places them in a mediating relationship with nature and sensuous activity (household labor, child-bearing, and child-rearing), their standpoint is "deeper-going" than the proletarian standpoint (1983, 234, 235-37). According to Hartsock, this feminist standpoint is mutually reinforced by the sexual division of labor in child-rearing and the "psychic experiences" produced by same-sex parenting (Hartsock 1983, 240).

As mentioned in the analysis of the role of standpoint in liberal feminism, universality is central to Hartsock's and Jaggar's conceptions of feminist standpoint. Theoretically, the antecedents can be traced from the abstract universality of the liberal polity through the economically-defined universality of the Marxist proletariat to the gender-defined universality of feminist standpoint theory's "woman." But, as indicated in the critique of the liberal standpoint, such universalizing claims also form a particular constellation of power which obtains legitimacy by ideologically erasing forms of repression and domination within the so-called universal group. The power of such universalizing claims is produced through the repression of difference. This has been a problem for Marxism, and it has been inherited by feminist standpoint theory.

In these works, both Jaggar and Hartsock are compelled to subsume and discount the differences and conflicts which mark relations between women in order to maintain a unitary feminist standpoint. Hartsock acknowledges that her analysis of the sexual division of labor "contains the danger of making invisible the experience of lesbians and women of color" but claims that the "effort to uncover a feminist standpoint assumes that there are some things common to all women's lives in Western class societies" (Hartsock 1983, 233-34). In prioritizing the category of gender, this formulation discounts the significance of racism and heterosexism and does not address the problems associated with analyzing the oppression of "Western" women removed from the contexts of colonialism and imperialism. Moreover, social class is also discounted when Hartsock argues that bourgeois women can also obtain an intensified "class consciousness" through household labor (1983, 236).

In "Postmodernism and Political Change," Hartsock (1990) engages this issue of universalism within feminist theory and indicates her approach to redressing the previous "exclusions" of that theory. Because Hartsock explicitly addresses the question of difference among women, this article is useful for clarifying some of the theoretical stakes in feminist standpoint theory. In the face of both the postmodern critique of epistemology and the institutionalization of "power by the ruling group," Hartsock asserts the importance of "situated knowledges" as the source of a "truer or more adequate account of reality" (1990, 25, 30). Although Hartsock retains what I believe to be the most significant contribution of feminist standpoint theory (the recognition of the power, of the counterhegemonic potential, associated with knowledge claims), she posits an organic relationship between experience and knowledge in which the latter "grows" from the former (Hartsock 1990, 24). In this analysis, knowledge "grows" from the experience of groups, but because the theoretical status of "groups" is not clarified, the derivation of experience from "group" allows for a creeping essentialism to enter the analysis.[10] Moreover, the undertheorized connection between experience and knowledge implies an immediate relationship between them. Because the project is cast in terms of "truer" knowledge, when Hartsock seeks to point out the political character of this knowledge, the problem becomes one not of political interpretation but of revelation. "[I]ntellectuals can be historically useful if they can . . . help to reveal collective identities" (Hartsock 1990, 27). In this epistemology, identity precedes experience, and knowledge follows closely from that "lived experience." The construction of identity as an interpretive and political process cannot be thematized by this approach to knowledge. Within Hartsock's conception of experience, knowledge and power, identity, even if more fragmented than the universalist "woman," still operates as an essentializing force. Further, the relations of power and domination between women are evaded in the pluralism of "situated knowledges." "Below" is not one space, not one depth.[11] The urge to theorize a commonality among women inhibits Hartsock's ability to acknowledge power differentials which constitute "difference." For example, the power relations between women are not addressed when "white feminist theory" is described as having merely "failed to include the situations of many women of color" (Hartsock 1990, 30-31).[12]

Similarly, Jaggar's analysis in *Feminist Politics and Human Nature* (1983), even as it seeks to address issues of power among women, subsumes differences among women within the universal "woman." "Whatever may be said about the position of peasants and people of color, feminist analysis has shown conclusively that the class analysis of traditional Marxism obscures important features of women's situation" (1983, 379). The positions of peasants and people of color are seen to be separate and distinct from the situation of "women." When explicitly addressing the challenge which women's social and political differences/conflicts present to a universalizing feminist standpoint theory, Jaggar states that a "representation of reality from the standpoint of women must draw on the variety of all women's experience" (Jaggar 1983, 387). But how can relations of political/social domination be cast as "variety"? Norma Alarcón points out that some of Jaggar's material in the closing section of the book is simply a restatement of positions articulated in *This Bridge Called My Back* (Alarcón 1990, 362). Jaggar does acknowledge these issues of difference, but they are not integrated into her analytical discussion of feminist standpoint theory. Thus, like Hartsock, Jaggar does not attribute adequate theoretical significance to the forms of power which inform and define relations between women.

This universalizing conception of gender is enacted through the scientific and objective quality of standpoint theory. As noted in the analysis of Marxist standpoint theory, women's standpoint theory, like Marxism, holds that its conception of women's subordination is objective. Both Jaggar and Hartsock emphasize the importance of analysis in achieving a feminist standpoint, which is "that perspective which reveals women's true interests and . . . is reached only through scientific and political struggle" (Jaggar 1983, 384). In spite of the emphasis on perspective, Jaggar's and Hartsock's theories of feminist standpoint seek to define a common vision of women's true interests. The call for scientific analysis complements the universalizing claims of feminist standpoint theory, by providing a method which, discounting the power relations among women, produces a common standpoint. The 1990 article by Hartsock, while it does not specifically address the question of standpoint, fails to consider this issue of power. Instead, Hartsock posits a plurality of "groups" and then identifies similarities among the knowledges of these various oppressed "groups" (Hartsock 1990, 26). In her recent comment on Susan Hekman's argument concerning feminist epistemology, Hartsock clarifies that standpoint theory addresses how knowledge claims operate to legitimate or critique established forms of power and notes that collective subjects or groups "must not be seen as formed unproblematically by existing in a particular social location" (1997, 371). Hartsock's arguments in this piece underscore the promise of standpoint theories as counterhegemonic, and also indicate a more complex treatment of collective identity. But the question of power in feminist standpoint theory is not adequately answered by making collective subject positions more "contingent." It is answered by addressing the forms of power involved in claiming a collective identity as the basis of knowledge. This involves, for example, grappling with race and racism in the formation of white women's experiences and knowledges. [13]

My purpose in working through Hartsock's and Jaggar's formulations of feminist standpoint theory is to focus attention on the forms of power operating to *produce* a collective subject position such as "women" or feminist. By analyzing Hartsock's and Jaggar's arguments, I have sought to clarify the problem of deriving knowledge claims *from* a "sociological" subject position. The alternative I explore and develop in the remainder of this paper seeks to avoid essentialism and to specify operations of power in standpoint theories by treating interpretations of experience and knowledge as processes which are *primary* to identity claims. This alternative seeks to rehabilitate identity as a political and interpretive, not objective and essentialist, category. As such, "identity," as a form of subjectivity, is a *product* of knowledge.

The versions of feminist standpoint theory I have discussed thus far cannot adequately conceptualize deep differences and conflicts between women in terms of their epistemological significance for standpoint theory. Chandra Mohanty's description of a politics of transcendence provides a succinct description of this theoretical problem:

the political is *limited to* the personal and all conflicts among and within women are flattened. If sisterhood itself is defined on the basis of personal intentions, attitudes or desires, conflict is also automatically constructed on only the psychological level. (Mohanty 1992, 82)

Given that feminist standpoint theory construes women's experience as leading to a universalized gender consciousness, Mohanty's concept of transcendence illuminates how such an understanding of experience severely limits possible forms of political action. Because it seeks a common standpoint (as primary) and a common understanding of experience as the basis of political solidarity, feminist standpoint theory ultimately relies upon a rigid conception of difference (absolute woman-man difference and ultimate woman-woman commonality) which sets in motion a logic of fragmentation. The proletariat as universal subject has been reconstituted as "woman," and faced with the failure of "woman" as a universal subject, what means has feminist standpoint theory for effectively engaging the subjectivities of its fractured Subject and forming an alternative politics?

CRITIQUES OF STANDPOINT THEORY: OBJECTIVITY AND SUBJECTIVITY

The logic of fragmentation contained within feminist standpoint theory is driven by claims to totalizing objective knowledge that are produced from a fixed subject position. Once the subject position ("woman") fails, this theory does not have resources to mediate more complex subjectivities. This is a logic of fragmentation because new and more specific fixed subject positions can be developed that make new and more specific claims to totalizing objective knowledge; but within the theoretical bounds of feminist standpoint theory, still no means of mediation would exist between these new fixed subjects and their objective knowledge claims. I present this logic of fragmentation through a temporal metaphor, but it is more accurately understood as a set of reinforcing tensions, operating simultaneously to enforce the limited and limiting vision of feminist standpoint theory. Lacking an understanding of difference which could include conflict and contestation among women, the theory discounts difference and emphasizes a universalizing conception of gender. Similarly, lacking a complex understanding of experience, the theory relies upon scientific practice to homogenize experience and produce totalizing objective knowledge.

Both Donna Haraway (1988) and Norma Alarcón (1990) provide critiques of feminist standpoint theory which challenge aspects of this logic. Haraway rejects the claims to totalizing knowledge and fixed subject position, arguing instead for partial knowledges and critical positionings. Alarcón challenges the relationship between subjectivity and knowledge which produces the authoritative and unitary subject of consciousness, arguing for a more nuanced "multiple-voiced" subjectivity. Though their critiques are distinct in important ways, both challenge the politics of transcendence promoted by feminist standpoint theory and explore the complexities which mark and divide women's experiences and knowledges.

In "Situated Knowledges: The Science Question in Feminism and the Privilege of Partial Perspective," Haraway (1988) breaks from feminist standpoint theory's logic of fragmentation by seeking a concept of objectivity which is not rooted in a fixed subject position. Defining objectivity as "critical positioning," Haraway embraces "situated and embodied knowledges" and rejects relativism as "a way of being nowhere while claiming to be everywhere" (586, 583, 584). Concerning those critical positions, Haraway acknowledges that "there is good reason to believe vision is better from below the brilliant space platforms of the powerful," but also argues that "the standpoints of the subjugated are not 'innocent' positions" (583, 584). She argues that "splitting, not being, is the privileged image for feminist epistemologies of scientific knowledge," and points out that:

> Only those occupying the positions of the dominators are self-identical, unmarked, disembodied, unmediated, transcendent, born again. It is unfortunately possible for the subjugated to lust for and even scramble into that subject position–and then disappear from view. (Haraway 1988, 586-87)

Haraway not only cautions against granting unexamined authority to subjugated knowledges but also warns of the "danger of romanticizing and/or appropriating the vision of the less powerful while claiming to see from their positions" (1988, 584). However, she does maintain that people can "learn to see faithfully from another's point of view" and, indeed, the possibility of such "critical positioning" is the basis of her view of objectivity (583).

For Haraway, feminist standpoint theory is too simplified and fixed. However, it does underscore the importance of "engaged, accountable positioning" (1988, 590). While she introduces several layers of complexity through her conception of partial knowledges and critical positioning, her concern for objectivity and her belief in the possibility of learning to "see faithfully from another's point of view" reflects a connection to the universalizing impulse of feminist standpoint theory. Through her concept of objectivity, Haraway provides a method to unify, at an epistemological level, "partial views and halting voices into a collective subject position" (1988, 590). While Haraway develops a more nuanced and less reductionist conception of objectivity than does feminist standpoint theory, it seems that she treats difference, in the final epistemological instance, as a problem to be overcome. The universalizing theoretical impulse is incompatible with a view of "difference" as autonomy; autonomous difference, defying objective perception, would threaten the epistemological project of objectivity.

While Alarcón shares Haraway's suspicion of the fixed subject position of feminist standpoint theory, her critique of hegemonic feminism's subject of consciousness also challenges the ways that Haraway's concept of objectivity reproduces assumptions about the compatibility of all subjectivities and the possibility of merging varying subjectivities into a "collective subject position." Alarcón's (1990) "The Theoretical Subject(s) of *This Bridge Called My Back* and Anglo-American Feminism" considers how the challenges raised to the hegemonic United States feminism practiced by bourgeois, white women have "yet to effect a newer discourse" (358). Analyzing how hegemonic feminists' counteridentification with white men "leaves us unable to explore relationships among women," Alarcón points out that the issues raised in *This Bridge Called My Back* have not been taken up as deep problems and concerns for conceptions of feminist subjectivity by Anglo-American feminists but, instead, have been superficially appropriated as "an instance of difference between women," without questioning the "unitary category of woman/women" (1990, 358-59). The deep structure of Anglo-American feminism privileges the subject of consciousness as its model of subjectivity. "The subject (and object) of knowledge is now a woman, but the inherited view of consciousness has not been questioned at all" (Alarcón 1990, 357).

Alarcón argues that a "logic of identification" with the dominant European/American masculine tradition "as a first step in constructing the theoretical subject of feminism is often veiled from standpoint epistemologists" because of the preoccupation with specifying how women are different from men (Alarcón 1990, 358). By focusing on "sexual difference" as the central issue, gendered power is constructed only in terms of white, bourgeois men. This obscures how gender also organizes power between women along simultaneous valences of nation, race, sexuality, and/or ethnicity ("one may also 'become a woman' in opposition to other women"). Moreover, gender organizes power between privileged women and marginalized men along similar valences, between men and women within marginalized or dominated communities, and in other complex ways including the forms of power between communities (Alarcón 1990, 360, 357-58). Such a worldview, which includes "other analytical categories such as race and class becomes impossible for a subject whose consciousness, refuses to acknowledge that 'one becomes a woman' in ways that are much more complex than in simple opposition to men" (Alarcón 1990, 360). In analyzing how standpoint theory has informed certain approaches to feminist ethnography, Kamala Visweswaran argues that standpoint perspectives "assume women are all members of the same 'sex' notwithstanding different gender identifications produced by culture" (Visweswaran, forthcoming). Alarcón (1990) indicates the implications of the counteridentifying stance adopted by feminist standpoint theory:

> However, this gendered standpoint epistemology, leads to feminism's bizarre position with regard to other liberation movements, working inherently against the interests of nonwhite women and no one else. (358)

Alarcón argues that feminism must move beyond the "oppositional theory of the subject" which grounds women's standpoint theory and calls for a "reconfiguration of the subject of feminist theory, and her relational position to a multiplicity of others, not just white men" (366, 359).

Such multiplicity is central to Alarcón's re-visioning of subjectivity. But this is not the thin version of plurality offered by much standpoint theory in which the heterogeneity of identity is recognized but denied at a theoretical level by "reconfirming a unified subjectivity or 'shared consciousness' through gender" (Alarcón 1990, 364). Instead, arguing that the theory of the subject of consciousness "is always already a posture of domination," Alarcón calls for a deep theory of "consciousness as a site of multiple voicings" (364, 365).

> Indeed the multiple-voiced subjectivity is lived in resistance to competing notions for one's allegiance or self-identification. It is a process of disidentification (see Pecheux 1982) with prevalent formulations of the most forcefully theoretical subject of feminism. (Alarcón 1990, 366)

By declaring the discourse of unity a mode of domination, Alarcón's critique of the unitary female subject of oppositional consciousness presented in feminist standpoint theory breaks the logic of fragmentation which preoccupied Jaggar, Hartsock, and Haraway. The "politics of unity" was only unifying for those women who already shared positions of significant political power. Thus, Alarcón's analysis seems to indicate the need for a double displacement: a shift in political aspirations from "unity" to "solidarity" and a conceptual move from a unitary subject of consciousness to a more complex, shifting, mediating consciousness or subjectivity.

While both Alarcón and Haraway criticize the fixed subject position of feminist standpoint theory, Haraway reproduces the problematic aspects of that theory's reductionist treatment of difference while Alarcón presses for a radically complex and heterogeneous conception of consciousness and identity. Whereas both theorists reject a politics of "transcendence," Haraway's "critical positioning" seems to me more abstract, more suspicious of claims to experience than Alarcón's "multiple-voiced" subjectivity. Thus I see Alarcón's critique of feminist standpoint theory as promising more effective positionings from which to pursue a politics of "engagement" and to conduct a war of position (Mohanty 1992, 86).

TRANSFORMING STANDPOINT THEORIES

Patricia Hill Collins and bell hooks seek to develop positions from which to effect radical, transformative politics by adapting versions of standpoint theory to analyze their own and others' social and political positions as African-American women. How do their versions of standpoint theory break from the problems of feminist standpoint theory as exemplified in the texts I have discussed? What is to be gained from Collins's treatment of standpoint? While hooks does not explicitly engage standpoint theory, how does her theoretical analysis of experience and knowledge clarify the importance of establishing the primacy of experience (as an interpretive category) for standpoint theory? While the self-reflexive particularity of the subject positions they hold meets Haraway's call for situated knowledges, do they adopt the counteridentifying stance which Alarcón criticizes and, thus, reproduce the project of universalizing knowledge which fails to refigure difference in more heterogeneous and nuanced ways? I will argue that both Collins and hooks seek to reclaim experience, as a political and interpretive category through standpoint theories which assert the autonomy of their collective identities. These are self-consciously political theories. As in the discussion of Marxism, collective identities are constellations of power based on privileging certain qualities and suppressing others. The key question for Collins and hooks is whether or not their versions of standpoint theory are, in Alarcón's terms, disidentifying or merely counteridentifying. By establishing the *autonomy* of experience, Collins' and hooks' distinct theoretical strategies indicate how standpoint theory can be rehabilitated as a counterhegemonic strategy of disidentification. My purpose in examining these authors' works is to identify the theoretical tools they provide for transforming feminist standpoint theory.

In "The Social Construction of Black Feminist Thought," Collins (1989) sets forth a Black feminist standpoint and an Afro-centric epistemology appropriate for articulating the knowledge claims of that standpoint (755).[14] Arguing that the "long-term and widely shared resistance among African-American women can only have been sustained by an enduring and shared standpoint," Collins identifies two features of that standpoint: Black women's particular economic and political status leads to "distinctive" experiences, and these experiences in turn "stimulate a distinctive Black feminist consciousness" (1989, 746, 747-48). The articulation of this standpoint requires an alternative epistemology whose "criteria for substantiated knowledge" and "methodological adequacy" will be compatible with the experiences and consciousness of Black women (Collins 1989, 755).

The political quality of this project is clear. Collins comments on the political implications of both a Black feminist standpoint and an Afrocentric epistemology. Pointing out that Black feminist thought "can encourage collective identity by offering Black women a different view of themselves and their world than that offered by the established social order," Collins (1989) also notes that while "alternative knowledge claims in and of themselves are rarely threatening to conventional knowledge," alternative epistemologies challenge "the basic process used by the powerful to legitimate their knowledge claims" (750, 773). She also emphasizes the particularity and autonomy of the Black feminist standpoint, stating that "living life as an African-American woman is a necessary prerequisite for producing Black feminist thought" (Collins 1989, 770).[15]

While the project here is explicitly political in its concern to develop an effective, self-sustaining position for Black women, Collins rejects the universalizing knowledge claims associated with women's standpoint theory:

> While it is tempting to claim that Black women are more oppressed than everyone else and therefore have the best standpoint from which to understand the mechanisms, processes, and effects of oppression, this simply may not be the case. (Collins 1990, 757)

Avoiding the "temptation" to make such universalizing knowledge claims sets Collins' project apart from the counteridentifying logic of women's standpoint theory. As well, the concern to create alternative forms and standards for knowledge indicates the counterhegemonic quality of this approach. In a sense, Collins' effort to articulate and specify the "fixed" subjectivity of Black women reproduces the "subject of consciousness" which Alarcón criticizes.[16] But this effort could also be interpreted as grappling with the complex subjectivity of African-American women and arguing for alternative theories of knowledge to accommodate that subjectivity. However, insofar as Collins seeks to articulate a collective identity for Black women, her efforts are inevitably marked by certain forms of power. This trade-off between complex subjectivity and the formation of collective identities for cultural and political practice is certainly vexed, but to avoid the forms of "repressive" power which organize collective identities is also to avoid the forms of culturally transformative, politically effective power such identities offer. Her analysis is most troubling, on the grounds of identity, when the status of the "group" becomes theoretically detached from an account of experience as an interpretive process; these moments indicate an essentialist conception of identity which posits identity as prior to and thereby defining for experience and knowledge.[17]

Theoretically, Collins' project clarifies how experience, knowledge and identity can be conceived as political categories. Her approach indicates how, when experience ("living life as an African-American woman") not identity is treated as primary, the status of knowledge as developing from the interpretation and representation of that experience becomes clearer. Collective identity is, thus, developed as a third moment of interpretation and representation, a moment of political, not "fixed," subjectivity.

In *Feminist Theory: From Margin to Center,* bell hooks analyzes the standpoint of black Americans by examining the literal, geographic, and metaphoric social marginality she experienced growing up in Kentucky. Like Collins, hooks argues that the experience of racist marginalization has provided her with "a particular way of seeing reality" which "focused attention on the center as well as the margin" (hooks 1984, ix). In her adult encounters with white elite feminists, hooks complains that "they do not understand, cannot even imagine, that black women, as well as other groups of women who live daily in oppressive situations, often acquire an awareness of patriarchal politics from their lived experience" (hooks 1984, 10). As hooks analyzes her experiences of marginality, conflicts with racist feminists, and awareness that she knew far more about white culture and history than white people knew of black culture and history, she develops a standpoint theory which emphasizes "lived experience" as a key component of an oppositional consciousness.

Making the strong claim that "Black women with no institutionalized 'other' that we may discriminate against, exploit, or oppress often have a lived experience that directly challenges the prevailing classist, racist social structure and its concomitant ideology," hooks asserts a version of standpoint theory in which black women's subject position as "most" marginal translates into a totalizing radical knowledge (hooks 1984, 15). Although this version of standpoint theory can be seen as similar to Collins' effort to articulate a progressive Black feminist collective identity, it also shares aspects of the universalizing, counteridentifying posture found in women's standpoint theory. However, the general tone of hooks' analysis emphasizes that black women have a "special vantage point" which can inform criticism but does not serve as, or aspire to be, a completely totalizing knowledge (hooks 1984, 15).

In a later work, *Yearning: Race, Gender, and Cultural Politics,* hooks (1990) addresses the importance of forming identity politics which avoid essentialism and offer more complex conceptions of black identity. Stating that "opposition is not enough," hooks wonders how to "create an oppositional worldview, a consciousness, an identity, a standpoint" that serves not only in political struggle, but also "enables creative, expansive self-actualization" (15). While hooks reflects upon the problem of essentializing identity politics prevalent in the 1960's black power movement, which "conformed to a modernist universalizing agenda," she asserts that "given a pervasive politic of white supremacy which seeks to prevent the formation of radical black subjectivity, we cannot cavalierly dismiss a concern with identity politics" (hooks 1990, 25, 26). Arguing that essentialism, not identity *per se,* is the problem, hooks points out that through a critique of essentialism, "we are empowered to recognize multiple experiences of black identity . . . which make diverse cultural productions possible" (hooks 1990, 29). She goes on to warn that if such diversity is not recognized, black identity can be reduced to two possibilities: "nationalist or assimilationist" (hooks 1990, 29). Thus, hooks seeks to reclaim and refigure black identity politics through a conception of experience which allows greater complexity and heterogeneity than previous "modern" versions of black identity and radical politics. Such transformed politics "means that we must and can rearticulate the basis for collective bonding" (hooks 1990, 29). Here hooks offers a formulation which connects complex subjectivity with the empowering potential of collective identities.

As well as trying to reconceive the relationship between experience and identity politics, hooks presses for a more complex treatment of knowledge. hooks treats knowledge as both an empowering assertion of collective identity ("I am moved by that confrontation with difference which takes place on new ground . . . where radical black subjectivity is *seen,* not overseen by any authoritative Other claiming to know us better than we know ourselves.") and as a way to create and preserve connections with others along and across the valences of identity ("Here again I am really talking about cultivating habits of being that reinforce awareness that knowledge can be disseminated and shared on a number of fronts.") (hooks 1990, 22, 30-31).

While both Collins and hooks effectively refigure standpoint theory to convey more particularized knowledge claims from more complex subjectivities than feminist standpoint theory, hooks' recent work offers an especially sensitive and rich exploration of the connections between experience, knowledge, identity and politics. These theorists' forms of standpoint theory assert the autonomy of their standpoints and the knowledge claims produced, while accepting the existence of, and possible solidarity with, knowledges from other standpoints. This approach, which sees difference as autonomous, challenges the view which treats difference as fragmentation and thus requiring homogenization (Jaggar and the Hartsock of *Money, Sex, and Power*) or translation (Haraway). The coercive character of the "fragmentation" approach to difference is clarified by the contrast to the approaches of hooks and Collins. Thus, in their versions of standpoint theory, Collins and hooks both manage to maintain their commitments to effectively engaged politics without merely reproducing hegemonic forms of power and subjectivity.

CONCLUSION: STANDPOINT, HOME AND COALITION

> In a coalition you have to give, and it is different from your home. You can't stay there all the time. You go to the coalition for a few hours and then you go back and take your bottle wherever it is, and then you go back and coalesce some more. (Reagon 1983, 359)

In "Coalition Politics: Turning the Century," Bernice Johnson Reagon (1983) addresses the relationship between "home," a place of nurturance and identification, and "coalition," a place of conflict and connection across identities (360). This distinction clarifies the moments of power operating in standpoint theories: the moment when experience, mediated through knowledge, is formed as some collective identity and the moment when that identity is articulated as an interpretation of politics, culture, and society. Reagon is ambivalent about this first moment, home. "[I]t's nurturing, but it is also nationalism" (358). In her analysis of Reagon's argument, Mohanty (1992) describes this phenomenon as "sameness in community . . . having been built on a debilitating ossification of difference" (85). As I have argued, hooks seeks to challenge this interpretation of community, arguing that essentialism need not be a defining feature of identity politics (hooks 1990, 20). Perhaps Caren Kaplan's (1987) conception of reterritorialization as a "place with room for what can be salvaged from the past and what can be made new" reflects this sense of a creative engagement with histories and traditions (194-95). However, for both hooks and Reagon, "home," the site of identification, is recognized as necessary yet distinct from other forms of politics.

Coalition is politics "in the streets" (Reagon 1983, 359). Mohanty (1992) interprets Reagon's call for coalition in terms of Gramsci's war of position. "Reagon's insistence on breaking out of barred rooms and struggling for coalition is a recognition of the importance–indeed the inevitable necessity–of wars of position" (85). Coalition is the second moment within standpoint theories when experience, knowledge, and identity form a position for effective political engagement.[18] Thus standpoint theories provide both a place to stand and a vantage point which reflect the mutually necessary moments of the war of maneuver and the war of position. Chela Sandoval's analysis of oppositional consciousness echoes this political interpretation of knowledge and identity.

> U.S. third world feminists must recognize that our learned sensitivity to the mobile webs of power is a skill that, once developed, can become a sophisticated form of oppositional consciousness. This is a form of oppositional consciousness which creates the opportunity for flexible, dynamic and tactical responses, it is another critical theory for political action which allows us no *single* conceptualization of our position in society. (1990, 66)

Experience can be claimed both as a site of "multiple voicings," as Alarcón has argued, and as a political site for the construction of critical, oppositional knowledges.

But experience as a political site does not exist within hegemonic, narrowly predefined categories of identity. Such oppositional consciousness, or in Gloria Anzaldúa's terms, *mestiza* consciousness, operates by challenging established and imposed boundaries of identity.

> The struggle is inner . . . our psyches resemble the bordertowns and are populated by the same people. The struggle has always been inner, and is played out in the outer terrains. Awareness of our

situation must come before inner changes, which in turn come before changes in society. Nothing happens in the "real" world unless it first happens in the images in our heads . . . I seek new images of identity, new beliefs about ourselves, our humanity and worth no longer in question. (1987, 87)

This theory of consciousness represents an epistemological challenge to interpretations of identity and knowledge which treat difference as mere empirical variation. In this epistemology of autonomous (not fragmented) difference, experience, knowledge, and identity are refigured in political terms, and the relationships between each moment are reconceived not as objective or "true" representations of reality but as transformative interpretations and articulations of subjectivity. Within such a feminist theory, the political relationships between women, which constitute "difference," cannot be easily transcended by "taking the standpoint of others" or by learning to "see faithfully from another's point of view" or by assimilating (rendering similar) the particular knowledges of various identity groups (Benhabib 1992, 145; Haraway 1988, 583; Hartsock 1990, 26).[19] Such theoretical moves work to reinforce hegemonic conceptions of subjectivity, identity, and difference, and to inhibit the development of more specific vocabularies for the analysis of power and an accountable politics of engagement.

As discussed in the introduction of this paper, the problem with standpoint theories, to which postmodern critics are particularly attuned, is that power, in its discursive and practical operations, is involved in claiming a collective identity position for oneself and others. But power is not just a "problem"; it also indicates that something is at stake. Thus, the formation of standpoint theories, while fraught with questions of knowledge, identity, and power, can contribute, as do the theories of Collins and hooks, to a transformative, empowering politics in which experience, when interpreted and constituted as knowledge, can provide authority for collective identity.[20] Such authority also allows for a theory of accountability whereby the interpretive and representational practices which constitute political knowledge can be specified and debated.

As I indicated in the introduction, this essay itself is fraught with issues and forms of power endemic to the process of myself, an economically, nationally and racially dominant woman, writing the thoughts and experiences of "subjugated" women. While I have formed "standpoint theory" as the subject of this essay, I have also tried to create a text in which these women's texts are also subjects, are recognized as autonomous of my own uses and interpretations. I have *written* this essay because I believe that experiences of marginality and domination, when transformed into identities, can have powerful political implications. *I* have written this essay because I believe that dominant elites must grapple with the implications of these power relations for their own politics and not easily resolve those power relationships into pluralist difference.

> Today wherever women gather together it is not necessarily nurturing. It is coalition building. And if you feel the strain, you may be doing some good work. (1983, 362)

—Bernice Johnson Reagon

NOTES

1. See also Evelyn Brooks Higginbotham (1992), whose focus on the operation of race difference and power destabilizes any essentialist conception of gender identity and who argues for a politicized and contingent interpretation of identity.

2. For a helpful discussion see the introduction to Hubert L. Dreyfus and Paul Rabinow (1982).

3. Such a move is also suggested in Chela Sandoval's discussion of the terms "women of color" and "Third World women" as coalitional, not essentialist, terms for political practice (Sandoval 1990, 62). See also, Joan Scott (1988, 88-90).

4. There are a range of positions concerning the capitalization of "black" and "white" in reference to racial identity. Particularly, "Black" can emphasize a collective political identity which is comparable to national identifications such as Irish, Irish American, Native American, Puerto Rican, Mexican, Mexican American, Chicana, and American. In writing this essay, I use these words to reflect existing racialized categories, and I see capitalizing "black" (or "white," though of course there are different issues involved with this term given its hegemonic status in a system of white supremacy) as reflecting a particular interpretation of political identity. As I argue in this paper, I believe the formation of political identities such as Black feminist or Black women (as well as others) is critical for an emancipatory and transformative politics.

5. In this paper I will use the term "feminist," as opposed to "women's," standpoint theory, although, as I acknowledge in my discussion of Nancy Hartsock's analysis of standpoint, the distinction between women's and feminist standpoint theory can be conceptually significant. I choose to use the term feminist standpoint theory because it highlights the political epistemology of the works I address and of my own theoretical project.

6. For discussions of accountable positioning, see Donna Haraway (1988) and Kamala Visweswaran (1994, 40-48).

7. For example, in another piece Okin argues that complete reasoning in the original position will not be possible "until the life experiences of the two sexes

become as similar as their biological differences permit" (Okin 1987, 72). By posing a conflict between a diversity of "life experiences" and universalism, Okin's approach ties a universalizable theory of justice to a unitary identity position. At the core, such a move treats difference as a problem to be overcome; further, it works to evade the conflicts and power hierarchies among women when the category of "gender" is privileged theoretically to those of "race" and "class." Within universalist moral theory, an alternative to Okin's conflation of universalism with a standpoint of sameness is Seyla Benhabib's notion of interactive universalism. The question remains, however, as to the epistemological status of difference for Benhabib (Benhabib 1987, 81).

8. Also see Hartsock's recent "Comment on Hekman's 'Truth and Method' " (1997, 268). In the tradition of the sociology of knowledge, Mannheim (1968) is another key figure for the analysis of standpoint.

9. For a brief account of the intellectual history of standpoint see Harding (1993, 53-54).

10. For an argument on the role of essentialism in social constructionist theories, see Fuss (1989).

11. Hartsock acknowledges Donna Haraway's influence on her own analysis of "situated knowledges" (Hartsock 1990, 23, fn.18). I will discuss Haraway's treatment of situated knowledges in the following section.

12. Another example of the essentialist treatment of identity occurs when postmodernism is defined as a situated knowledge of a "particular group–Euro-American, masculine, and racially as well as economically privileged" (Hartsock 1990, 23). The work of feminist theorists, from diverse racial, ethnic and national locations, who are creatively challenging, changing and developing theory within the broad parameters of postmodernism, is not just ignored but rendered definitionally incompatible with some presumed identity and experience.

13. For a powerful and incisive analysis of how race and racism informs and effects experience, knowledge and political practice from a position of white racial privilege, see Segrest (1994).

14. For a more extensive treatment, see also Collins (1990).

15. Collins also emphasizes this point in "Comment on Hekman's 'Truth and Method: Feminist Standpoint Theory Revisited': Where's the Power?" (1997, 375-376).

16. Higginbotham makes a related criticism of Collins' standpoint approach: "Notwithstanding the critical importance of this work in contesting racism and sexism in the academy and larger society, its focus does not permit sufficient exploration of ideological spaces of difference among black women themselves" (Higginbotham 1992, 270-71). For example, see Collins (1997, 377).

17. For example: "Standpoint theory argues that groups who share common placement in hierarchical power relations also share common experiences in such power relations. Such shared angles of vision lead those in similar social locations to be predisposed to interpret these experiences ina comparable fashion." But also note that Collins continues: "The existence of the group as the unit of analysis

neither means that all individuals within the group have the same experiences nor that they interpret them in the same way" (Collins 1997, 377).

18. Hartsock echoes this concern for alliances when she states: "Most importantly, I believe that the task facing all progressive theorists is that of trying to expose and clarify the theoretical bases for political alliance and solidarity" (Hartsock 1990, 24).

19. Iris Young's theory of group difference and representation is another example of a strategy for recognizing political difference which I believe operates to institutionalize dominant conceptions of identity. In terms of theories of justice, however, I would suggest that the concept of accountability offers a foothold for the theorization of justification procedures (Young 1989).

20. Addressing women of color as to the importance of developing theoretical knowledges, Gloria Anzaldúa explains: "Because we are not allowed to enter discourse, because we are often disqualified and excluded from it, because what passes for theory these days is forbidden territory for us, it is *vital* that we occupy theorizing space, that we not allow white men and women solely to occupy it. By bringing in our own approaches and methodologies, we transform that theorizing space" (Anzaldúa 1990, xxv).

REFERENCES

Alarcón, Norma. 1990. "The Theoretical Subject(s) of *This Bridge Called My Back* and Anglo-American Feminism." In *Making Face, Making Soul: Haciendo Caras,* ed. Gloria Anzaldúa. San Francisco: Aunt Lute Foundation.

Anzaldúa, Gloria. 1987. *Borderlands/La Frontera: The New Mestiza.* San Francisco: Spinsters/Aunt Lute.

Barrett, Michèle, and Anne Phillips. 1992. "Introduction." In *Destabilizing Theory: Contemporary Feminist Debates,* ed. Michèle Barrett and Anne Phillips. Stanford: Stanford University Press.

Benhabib, Seyla. 1987. "The Generalized and the Concrete Other: The Kohlberg-Gilligan Controversy and Feminist Theory." In *Feminism as Critique: On the Politics of Gender,* ed. Seyla Benhabib and Drucilla Cornell. Minneapolis: University of Minnesota Press.

Benhabib, Seyla. 1992. *Situating the Self: Gender, Community and Postmodernism in Contemporary Ethics.* New York: Routledge.

Benhabib, Seyla. 1995. "Feminism and Postmodernism: An Uneasy Alliance." In *Feminist Contentions: A Philosophical Exchange.* ed. Seyla Benhabib, Judith Butler, Drucilla Cornell, and Nancy Fraser, New York: Routledge.

Benhabib, Seyla, Judith Butler, Drucilla Cornell, and Nancy Fraser. 1995. *Feminist Contentions: A Philosophical Exchange.* New York: Routledge.

Collins, Patricia Hill. 1989. "The Social Construction of Black Feminist Thought." *Signs* 14:745-73.

Collins, Patricia Hill. 1990. *Black Feminist Thought: Knowledge, Consciousness, and the Politics of Empowerment.* Boston: Unwin Hyman.

Collins, Patricia Hill. 1997. "Comment on Hekman's 'Truth and Method: Feminist Standpoint Theory Revisited': Where's the Power?" *Signs* 22:375-81.

Dreyfus, Hubert L., and Paul Rabinow. 1982. *Michel Foucault: Beyond Structuralism and Hermeneutics.* Chicago: University of Chicago Press.

Fuss, Diana. 1989. *Essentially Speaking: Feminism, Nature and Difference.* New York: Routledge.

Haraway, Donna. 1988. "Situated Knowledges: The Science Question in Feminism and the Privilege of Partial Perspective." *Feminist Studies* 14:575-99.

Harding, Sandra. 1993. "Rethinking Standpoint Epistemology: What is 'Strong Objectivity?' " In *Feminist Epistemologies,* ed. Linda Alcoff and Elizabeth Potter. New York: Routledge.

Hartsock, Nancy. 1983. *Money, Sex, and Power: Toward a Feminist Historical Materialism.* New York: Longman.

Hartsock, Nancy. 1990. "Postmodernism and Political Change: Issues for Feminist Theory." *Cultural Critique* (14):15-33.

Hartsock, Nancy. 1997. "Comment on Hekman's 'Truth and Method: Feminist Standpoint Theory Revisited': Truth or Justice?" *Signs* 22:367-74.

Hekman, Susan. 1997. "Truth and Method: Feminist Standpoint Theory Revisited." *Signs* 22:341-65.

Higginbotham, Evelyn Brooks. 1992. "African-American Women's History and the Metalanguage of Race." *Signs* 17:251-74.

hooks, bell. 1984. *Feminist Theory: From Margin to Center.* Boston: South End Press.

hooks, bell. 1990. *Yearning: Race, Gender, and Cultural Politics.* Boston: South End Press.

Jaggar, Alison. 1983. *Feminist Politics and Human Nature.* New Jersey: Rowman and Allanheld.

Kaplan, Caren. 1987. "Deterritorializations: The Rewriting of Home and Exile in Western Feminist Discourse." *Cultural Critique* (6):187-98.

Lukács, Georg. 1971. *History and Class Consciousness: Studies in Marxist Dialectics.* Cambridge: MIT Press.

Mannheim, Karl. 1968. *Ideology and Utopia: An Introduction to the Sociology of Knowledge.* New York: Harcourt, Brace & World.

Mohanty, Chandra. 1992. "Feminist Encounters: Locating the Politics of Experience." In *Destabilizing Theory: Contemporary Feminist Debates,* ed. Michèle Barrett and Anne Phillips. Stanford: Stanford University Press.

Nicholson, Linda. 1990. "Introduction." In *Feminism/Postmodernism,* ed. Linda Nicholson. New York: Routledge.

Okin, Susan Moller. 1987. "Justice and Gender." *Philosophy and Public Affairs* 16:42-72.

Okin, Susan Moller. 1989. "Reason and Feeling in Thinking About Justice." *Ethics* 99:229-49.

Pecheux, Michel. 1982. *Language, Semantics and Ideology.* New York: St. Martin's Press.

Reagon, Bernice Johnson. 1983. "Coalition Politics: Turning the Century." In

Home Girls: A Black Feminist Anthology, ed. Barbara Smith. New York: Kitchen Table: Women of Color Press.

Sandoval, Chela. 1990. "Feminism and Racism: A Report on the 1981 Women's Studies Association Conference." In *Making Face, Making Soul: Haciendo Caras,* ed. Gloria Anzaldúa. San Francisco: Aunt Lute Foundation.

Scott, Joan. 1988. *Gender and the Politics of History.* New York: Columbia University Press.

Segrest, Mab. 1994. *Memoir of a Race Traitor.* Boston: South End Press.

Visweswaran, Kamala. 1994. *Fictions of Feminist Ethnography.* Minneapolis: University of Minnesota Press.

Visweswaran, Kamala. N.d. "Histories of Feminist Ethnography." *Annual Review of Anthropology.* Forthcoming.

Young, Iris. 1989. "Polity and Group Difference: A Critique of the Ideal of Universal Citizenship." *Ethics* 99:250-74.

Feminist Standpoint
as Postmodern Strategy

Nancy J. Hirschmann

SUMMARY. Postmodern critiques of standpoint theory have been particularly influential in feminist theory, but I maintain that they are often mistaken. In this essay, I will briefly review the most common criticisms and show how Hartsock's formulation addresses many of them and indeed shares many features of postmodernism through the notion of multiple feminist standpoints. Though several feminists have urged such pluralization, I identify a more intractable difficulty with such a strategy and argue for a new way of conceptualizing the "materialist" dimensions of "experience" that may be more palatable to postmodern notions of discursiveness without giving away Hartsock's methodological foundation. *[Article copies available for a fee from The Haworth Document Delivery Service: 1-800-342-9678, E-mail address: getinfo@haworth.com]*

In the approximately 15 years since Nancy Hartsock published "The Feminist Standpoint" (1983),[1] this epistemological methodology has had a profound affect on feminist theorizing and scholarship in a variety of fields ranging from philosophy (Ruddick 1989, Alcoff and Potter 1993), social work (Swigonski 1994), sociology (McLennon 1995, Ramazanoglu 1989, Smith 1990, Collins 1990), psychology (Henwood and Pidgeon 1995), and history (Offen 1990), to geography (McDowell 1992), and the biological and physical sciences (Harding 1986, 1991, Keller 1985). Within political science, it has had a significant impact not only on Hartsock's own field of political theory (Flax 1983, Hirschmann 1989, 1992, Jagger

[Haworth co-indexing entry note]: "Feminist Standpoint as Postmodern Strategy." Hirschmann, Nancy J. Co-published simultaneously in *Women & Politics* (The Haworth Press, Inc.) Vol. 18, No. 3, 1997, pp. 73-92; and: *Politics and Feminist Standpoint Theories* (ed: Sally J. Kenney and Helen Kinsella) The Haworth Press, Inc., 1997, pp. 73-92. Single or multiple copies of this article are available for a fee from The Haworth Document Delivery Service [1-800-342-9678, 9:00 a.m. - 5:00 p.m. (EST). E-mail address: getinfo@haworth.com].

73

1983, Weeks 1995) but on public policy (Rixecker 1994) and international relations as well (Keohane 1989, Sylvester 1994).

At the same time, indeed perhaps because of this powerful influence, feminist standpoint theory has been subject to considerable criticism and contentious debate within feminism. The postmodern critique of standpoint theory has been particularly strong and fairly consistent. But I believe it is often mistaken. In this essay, I will briefly review the most common criticisms and show how Hartsock's formulation not only addresses many of them but shares important features with postmodernism as well. Though several feminists, including myself, have argued for a postmodern potential in the notion of multiple feminist standpoints, I carry this further to argue for a new way of conceptualizing the materialist dimensions of experience that may be more compatible with postmodern notions of discursivity without losing Hartsock's methodological foundation.

Essentially Universal?

Essentialism and universalism are the charges most commonly leveled against feminist standpoint theory, though not exclusively by postmodernists by any means. It is often held that Hartsock claimed to articulate "the" feminist standpoint, as if there were only one, and that it was the same for all women. Such universalist "truth-claims," the criticism goes, are based on ahistorical, crosscultural effects that link "women" to each other regardless of other identity aspects of culture, ethnicity, race, sexuality, or class (hooks 1984, Spelman 1988) and simply replace one set of universal claims for another, thus replicating and reinscribing the hegemony it seeks to displace (Flax 1990, Hekman 1990). At the same time, anti-essentialist critics have accused Hartsock of basing the standpoint on biology, reproduction, or "nature" (Fraser and Nicholson 1990, Grant 1993).

Such criticisms have fostered lively debates within feminism concerning the "meaning of woman" and the "subject" of feminism that go well beyond the immediate methodological and political concerns of Hartsock's argument. They have highlighted the ways in which largely white-dominated academic feminism has often worked to exclude the experiences and views of U.S. women of color, poor women, Third World women, and lesbians (Narayan 1989, Collins 1990). These debates have forced feminism to examine itself, to be more self-conscious, self-aware, and self-critical in developing its analyses and theories, and to attend more consistently to its avowed goals of equality and inclusion.

At the same time, however, such criticisms are often unfair to Hartsock.

The charge of essentialism, for instance, ignores the fact that Hartsock locates her conception of a feminist standpoint in the culturally constructed social relations of household production and reproduction in late capitalism (Hartsock 1984, 234-40). It may be true that the practices Hartsock bases her feminist standpoint on are grounded in biology in a certain sense: for instance, the human need to eat means that we have to provide food for ourselves; and the development of human personality, psyche, emotions, and intellect requires some kind of adult caretaking of human infants. But this hardly precludes historical analysis: indeed, a feminist standpoint allows us to answer why it is that *women* have been responsible for providing for these needs in most cultures and historical periods. The social construction of experience, and particularly labor (Hartsock 1983, 283), is a critical aspect of Hartsock's approach (see also Ferguson 1993).

To this end, in contrast to some other theorists such as Dorothy Smith (1990) and Nel Noddings (1990), who have written in terms of "women's" stand-points, Hartsock explicitly distinguishes between "female" and "feminist" standpoints (Hartsock 1984, 232). This distinction is due partly to an overt political commitment to the notion that there can be, must be, and indeed currently are male feminists in the world; but it is also due to her central contention that a standpoint does not come "naturally" or spontaneously to anyone. Rather, it must be achieved through "struggle," wherein lies its "liberatory" potential (Hartsock 1983, 235). As Sandra Harding (1991) has asserted in defense of standpoint theory, its goal is not to "act out" women's experiences but to theorize them critically and to learn about women's responses to oppression as much as about oppression itself.

Of course, as Kathy Ferguson (1993) has noted, many anti-essentialist critiques are really criticisms of univeralism, not "essentialism per se" (81-82), and this distinction is important. Charges of "universalism" often misrepresent Hartsock's position as well. Indeed, in one of her early formulations of a feminist standpoint approach, Hartsock (1981) states explicitly that

> Women who call themselves feminists disagree on many things. . . . One would be hard pressed to find a set of beliefs or principles, or even a list of demands, that could safely be applied to all feminists. Still . . . there is a *methodology* common among feminists that differs from the practice of most social movements, particularly from those in advanced capitalist countries. At bottom, *feminism is a mode of analysis, a method of approaching life and politics, rather than a set*

of political conclusions about the oppression of women. (35-6, emphasis added)

The notion of standpoint as a methodology is crucial. Universalist criticisms confuse Hartsock's particular time-and context-bound contingent account of what "a" (as in "one") feminist standpoint might look like for the *conception* of "feminist standpoint theory" that she develops as a *method* for feminism. The central notion of a standpoint approach, as Hartsock develops it, is that material experience shapes epistemology. Hence, to the degree that people share a particular set of experiences, for instance, if large numbers of women have exclusive responsibility for raising children or perform uncompensated household labor for men, then they may share a standpoint. But by the same token, to the degree that experience differs, as childrearing practices do from culture to culture, then standpoints will differ as well. The particulars of experience may be historically contingent, but their methodological similarities cross over these contingencies. The methodological similarity provides the means for women within various groups to resist their oppression by drawing on the epistemological power their particular shared experiences affords to rename those experiences. That each group may realize its own substantively distinct standpoint, in response to the particular differences in the forms oppression takes for women of different races, classes, or sexualities, does not undermine this methodological commonality.

Missing this methodological point leads to misunderstanding. For instance, Vicky Spelman (1988) criticizes standpoint theory for its supposed "plethorophobia" of differences among women evidenced by its "hegemonic" tendency to seek commonality among women, which she asserts is impossible. "Is there some*thing* all women have in common. . . . *An* underlying identity as women. . . . *A* shared viewpoint?" (160, my emphasis). Similarly, Judith Grant (1993) faults feminist standpoint epistemology because it does not "tell us *which* aspects of the lives of women count as epistemologically important. . . . which parts of our lives and experiences are endemic to our being female. Therefore the epistemological question is precisely the one avoided" (100).

But Grant sets up the very problem for which she most excoriates standpoint theory: confusing a feminist standpoint with the essential experience of "being female" while simultaneously ignoring that Hartsock does in fact point to specific aspects of women's experience, namely unpaid household labor and reproduction in the broad sense of caregiving and nurturance. Spelman seems to lock Hartsock into a circle of her own creation: in order to be valid, feminist standpoint must be the same for all women; in order to be the same, experience must also be the same either through biological mandate or a universal construction; but experience is not the same; therefore, standpoint is wrong.[2]

But if we see instead that the *process* of developing a standpoint is similar, though the substance of particular standpoints will differ according to experience, then we see that the feminist standpoint approach readily accommodates difference, specificity, and history. The epistemological point is the methodological one: it refers to the general process of how knowledge is to be developed and understood. Epistemology is not a theory of *what* we know, but of *how* we know it. While standpoint feminism has been instrumental in highlighting the interactions of "what" and "how," the two are not identical. That is, if knowledge is developed through experience rather than in the abstract world of "Truth," then different experiences will yield different *bodies of knowledge.* However, the process of *developing knowledge out of* these different experiences will be similar for all. By focusing on standpoint as a methodological and epistemological strategy rather than a particular political positioning, Hartsock's formulation allows for a multiplicity of feminist *standpoints.*

Several theorists (e.g., Haraway 1991, Harding 1991, Hirschmann 1992) have argued precisely this point. Pluralizing the term to feminist *standpoints* allows the recognition of difference, particularity, and context while also putting certain parameters on what can count as a *feminist* standpoint. These parameters do not entail some universal and timeless conception of feminism or femaleness; rather, "feminism" is the product of ongoing political negotiation within and among various groups of women who theorize from the standpoint of their experiences of gender, race, class, and other oppressions. The materialist basis of feminist standpoint theory leads logically to the conclusion that differences in experience produce differences in standpoints; the pluralization of feminist standpoints recognizes differences among material experiences of women across history, race, class, and culture.

Feminism/Postmodernism

Even so, anti-universalist criticisms seem more persistent than anti-essentialist ones because they are based on the "logic" of standpoint arguments rather than a simple misreading: standpoint feminism does require shared group experiences. Although some theorists such as Collins (1990) have written of a "self-actualized standpoint," it is a central aspect of Hartsock's formulation that a feminist standpoint can only arise within circumstances of *shared oppression.* In keeping with its Marxist and Lukacian heritage, a standpoint is not simply a "perspective" or "point of view," which can vary from person to person, but is rather an epistemology, which must be shared between at least some numbers of people and which is a function of political struggle with other people who are similarly placed vis-à-vis oppressive power relations (Hartsock 1997). This may allow difference *among* groups, but it requires similarity *within* "epistemological communities" (Seller 1994).

Thus, an unmodified "feminist" standpoint logically presupposes an unmodified group of "women" who share similar experiences. This is not an exclusively postmodern criticism. Feminists-of-color are particularly critical of the way that standpoint's universalist potential has been unwittingly promoted by many white feminists through such usage of the term "feminist standpoint" rather than more specified terms such as "Black feminist standpoint" or "white feminist standpoint" (Mohanty 1992). Such criticisms are valid. When Hartsock tables the question of race to talk about "commonalities" in *Money, Sex and Power* (1984, 233), she ignores that race and class affect the gendered constructions of the very labor activities on which she wants to base her particular instance of a feminist standpoint.

While such substantive exclusions seriously undermine feminism, they do not mean that standpoint as a method is fundamentally irreconcilable with the lives of women of color or with the notion of "difference" more generally. Indeed, Collins (1990) and Narayan (1989) have argued that standpoint feminism provides an important method for developing feminist-of-color standpoints. This may be one place where feminism-of-color and postmodernism part company. Although feminist postmodernism has helped open up white academic feminism to questions of racism, classism, and other exclusions that are not only harmful to many women but also contradict and undermine feminism, it nevertheless maintains that it is logically impossible to reconcile standpoint theory with "difference." Postmodernists note that every modifier has its own universalistic potential; thus even a "Black feminist standpoint" does not sufficiently attend to differences among Black women's experiences in terms of class or sexuality (Spelman 1988). While a standpoint approach may be consistent with multiplicity, particularizing can get us only so far before difference runs up against the standpoint requirement of sharedness.

By emphasizing the ways in which language and "discourse" construct categories of meaning to create the "realities" of "who we are," feminist postmodernists point out the dangers in using terms like "women" such that feminists unintentionally silence or erase women of color or poor women who do not make up the majority of feminist theorists. At the same time, however, many feminists believe that postmodernism's continual contestation of identity as a contingent and fleeting construction of language threatens the central project of standpoint feminism (if not "feminism" in general) which is to secure the acknowledgement that various groups of "women" are oppressed in concrete ways.

The particulars of the often bitter and passionate debate over feminist postmodernism will not be rehearsed here (see Alcoff 1988, Hawksworth 1989), but this debate has created a strong ambivalence among many feminist scholars who seek a methodological strategy for studying "women." As Caroline Ramazanoglu (1989) notes, "reducing feminism to a post-modern philosophy excises feminist politics" and leads to "the political fragmentation of feminist strategies for change." Yet at the same time, she worries that a standpoint approach requires an epistemological and political unity among all women (432, 438). The apparent conflict between embracing and addressing "difference" among women and yet being able to hold onto a concept of "woman" which retains some conception of commonality across various differences leaves many feminists who are attracted to standpoint theory on the horns of a seemingly irresolvable dilemma.

While some might celebrate such irresolvability, including some standpoint sympathizers (e.g. Harding 1991, Haraway 1991), I believe that the notion of multiple feminist standpoints holds an answer to this dilemma in what it reveals about the methodological significance of standpoint as *epistemological.* As a way of seeing the world, redefining knowledge, reconceptualizing social relations, and renaming experience, standpoint theory provides a powerful methodology for understanding "reality" as an ongoing process. That is, the adoption of a particular feminist standpoint allows us to gain a "less partial and perverse" understanding of the world; but that does not mean we have achieved "truth." To begin with, the confluence of a variety of feminist standpoints reveals different *aspects* of "truth," different angles on achieving clarity, different pieces of a larger picture (Haraway 1991). But in turn each of these standpoints, separately and working together, allows a reconfiguration of the world as a whole which, presumably, should lend itself to other subsequent standpoints that are even *less* "partial and perverse." Standpoint is, true to its Marxian roots, an ongoing, dialectical process (contra Grant 1993, 115).

A focus on multiple standpoints reveals standpoint and postmodernism as more closely related than many want to admit; it suggests that standpoint indeed is "always already" a postmodern strategy. Admittedly, this claim might seem counterintuitive, given views such as those expressed by Ramazanoglu, and particularly given Hartsock's own steady and repeated criticisms of such leading and diverse postmodern theorists as Foucault and Rorty (Hartsock 1987, 1990). Furthermore, standpoint theory's Marxist legacy would seem to locate it squarely within modernism.

But it is a view that a number of feminists have put forth, some implicitly, others explicitly. Donna Haraway argues that we need to see a standpoint as offering only a "partial perspective" that is compatible with both multiplicity and "successor science projects" without sliding into either relativism or totalization (1991, 191). Christine Sylvester's defense of standpoint theory for international relations points out that feminist standpoint's giving voice to "so many different experiences of so many different types of people called women," resonates with postmodernists' concern to reveal "the power and politics laden in local acts of resistance to universalising narratives" (1994, 324). Sandra Harding (1991) argues that standpoint theory's location in "women's lives" can help feminists theorize the "permanent partiality" of knowledge. Following Harding and Edward Said, Kathleen Lennon (1995) has argued for a "contrapuntal" approach to standpoint that both "highlights specificity and allows for the recognition of communalities" (141). I have elsewhere argued for seeing standpoint as a kind of "postmodern feminism," to be distinguished from "feminist postmodernism" (Hirschmann 1992).

Certainly, standpoint theory shares many features and goals with postmodernism. Postmodernism challenges the notion, central to modern political theory, that there is such a thing as "human nature." By emphasizing the notions of difference, particularity, and context, postmodernism seeks to shake us loose from modernist tendencies to make broad-sweeping generalizations that reflect particular historico-cultural locations, but which we try to pass off as "truth." Instead of having "natures," postmodern theory recognizes that we are "socially constructed." The idea of social construction central to postmodern theory suggests that we are who we are not because of "nature" but because of the social relations, institutions, and practices that shape our world. Our selfhood, subjectivity, identity, and way of seeing are all "constructed" by the contexts in which we live.

By challenging the naturalness of practices, social arrangements, and institutions, both standpoint theory and postmodernism see identity as socially constructed by particular historical and cultural contexts. As indicated earlier, the logic of materialism on which the feminist standpoint is based demands recognition that the structures of these activities have changed over time and differ across cultures, reflecting that they are in part the result of and responses to different forms of patriarchy in different cultures and different historical periods (Hartsock 1984, 150). Additionally, feminist standpoint theory explicitly acknowledges the ways in which the activities that women engage in have been for the most part assigned to them by men rather than "monopolized" by women (Hartsock 1984, 245).

Moreover, by providing a different approach to *epistemology,* feminist standpoint theory, like postmodernism, enables us to get beyond the superficial idea of "social construction" contained in such ideas as role learning or socialization. Humans are constructed not merely through quasi-conscious processes of learning sexist definitions of what a "woman" or "man" is within neutral conceptual vocabularies, linguistic forms, and frameworks for knowledge; rather, these latter profoundly affect, shape, and even determine the kinds of ideas, concepts, and visions of the self that are possible to conceive (Butler 1990). For instance, a feminist standpoint enables women to identify the activities they perform in the home as "work" and "labor," productive of "value," rather than simply the necessary and essential byproducts of "nature" or the function of biology which women "passively" experience (Hartsock 1984, 146-8). Such recognition involves a reconfiguring of meaning and discourse and not "just" a challenge to existing social relations of (re)production.

Feminist Standpoint and the Materialist Moment

Thus standpoint theory and feminist postmodernism share important features. However, this does not circumvent a deeper division between them, namely the *meaning* of "material reality" on which standpoint feminism is based and "discourse," central to postmodernism. Feminist postmodernists argue that we must give up any idea of a "material reality" that exists beyond discourse, that has an independent or objective status, otherwise we simply get caught by the very same essentialist and reductive assumptions that feminism was supposed to unmask in the first place. Feminist standpoint theorists want to assert that women's oppression is "real" and that it has an immediate, even tangible quality that pre-exists its naming in language. Indeed, the power of a standpoint is precisely its ability *to* name experiences that previously were defined in masculinist terms which made women's harm invisible.

But because such experiences *are* socially constructed, and because women are also located in other identity networks such as race and class, feminism also needs to engage discursivity as a way to appreciate how this invisibility operates and to understand the relationship of gender oppression to other forms of domination. In an essay otherwise critical of postmodernism, Mary Hawksworth (1989) faults standpoint theory because it "fails to grasp the manifold ways in which all human experiences . . . are mediated by theoretical presuppositions embedded in language and culture" (544). "Discourse" is not simply words, but a social force that sets the terms for the construction of material "reality." If "experience itself reflects and is partially constructed out of the self-understandings yielded by the imaginary and symbolic dimensions of our conceptual apparatus" (Lennon 1995, 135), then standpoint theory must recognize the discursive construction of the material experiences on which feminist standpoints are partially based.

This might suggest an insurmountable impasse: many would argue that once one concedes the importance of discourse, the notion of "prediscursivity" becomes unintelligible. But the word "partially" in the previous quote is crucial to avoiding a vicious circle. If feminists can understand women's experiences *solely* through discourses premised not only on women's oppression but on making that oppression invisible by naturalizing it, then it might seem that the basis for feminist standpoints evaporates. Standpoint feminism needs to hang onto at least some notion of "material reality" that is not entirely captured by discourse, as a way to hold onto the very concrete, immediate, and daily ways in which women suffer from the use and abuse of power specifically by men. However, this is precisely where the link between standpoint and postmodernism breaks down; even positing multiple standpoints is not enough to bring these two theoretical frameworks together. For postmodernists, it begs the question of whether *any* kind of standpoint simply reinscribes the old oppressions of truth and identity because the notion of an unmediated "experience" is by definition impossible. At the same time, the denial of such immediacy prompts standpoint theorists to fear a relativist erosion of the ability to make useful claims about women's oppression.

Rosemary Hennessy (1993) argues that the solution to this apparent impasse is for feminism to link the discursive to the nondiscursive (36), but so far, this link has only been one way, viz. acknowledging the ways in which discourse constructs the material conditions of women's lives, as even postmodernists like Judith Butler acknowledge. Butler (1993) claims that she does not dispute "the materiality of the body" but insists on the need to explore "the normative conditions under which the materiality of the body is framed and formed" (17). Her argument that "regulatory norms" are what "materialize" sex coheres with feminist standpoint's social constructivist arguments that the dominant ideology of patriarchy establishes and creates the reality of women's experience (e.g., Hartsock 1983, 288). Discourse makes "real," or "materializes," the concrete conditions of women's lives.

At the same time, however, the postmodern reiteration that "materiality is a function of discourse" begs the question for standpoint feminism, which wants to say that materiality can *challenge* discourse: that women's experience simultaneously sits *in contradiction to* discourse with a partially independent reality. This is a notion that postmodernists like Butler overtly reject; and yet Butler's use of the term "queer" as an empowering political positioning depends on precisely such notions (1993, 223). Gay and lesbian adoption of the term "queer" involves an ironic parodying of the dominant discourse, and its power lies in the fundamental belief that heteropatriarchy misunderstands and misdescribes gays and lesbians. The notion of "misdescription" presupposes a further notion of what they really are and that the dominant discourse "gets it wrong."

This suggests that we must not only see how discourse "materializes" experience but also acknowledge how material conditions construct and shape discourse. The problem, then, is how to make such a notion of a "prediscursive reality" intelligible within postmodern discursivity. To this end, I propose what I call a "materialist moment" that can serve as an interface between the possibility of a prediscursive "concrete reality" on which standpoint feminism logically depends and the postmodern emphasis on the constantly shifting discursive character of such "reality." The notion of a "moment" comes out of postmodern theory to indicate a disjunction between discourses, a figurative "moment" in time where individuals see that the existing dominant discourse is not "true." This moment need not be literally "momentary"; that is, moments do not necessarily last for just a few seconds but can mark historical epochs of transformation or shifting between dominant and resisting discourses. It is a "moment" of, and in the development of, consciousness, both individual and collective, which must change continually in response to historical events, even when it appears stable or static. Within the human mind, it may more literally be momentary, an almost instantaneous recognition that must immediately slide away into discourse and representation.[3]

For instance, Drucilla Cornell (1993, 102-10) writes about a "utopian moment" where (following the French feminists) women's sexual *jouissance* can express itself outside of the patriarchal context and language that defines women's sexuality only as "that which is fucked." It is "utopian" because Cornell recognizes the impossibility of this *jouissance* ever having meaning outside of language; but it is a "moment" to affirm the fleeting recognition of women's experiencing of their own bodily sexuality in a way not wholly contained by discourse, evaporating even as it comes into being.

The materialist moment works off of a similar notion. In her early writings, Hartsock (1983) seems to acknowledge the paradoxical relationship between discourse and materiality when she admits to "grasping [bodily experience] over-firmly . . . to keep it from evaporating altogether" (289). It may be this "over-firmness" that leads to the essentialist and universalist criticisms earlier cited, but it stems from her recognition of the fact that women's "experience" already exists within patriarchal discourse (Hartsock 1984, 245). Indeed, this is why a feminist standpoint yields "less partial and perverse" knowledge rather than "truth." Hartsock's point, however, is that this discursive construction is not and cannot be the sum total of women's experience. "Sensuous human activity" (Hartsock 1983, 235), materiality, underlies such construction and awaits its articulation in a new discourse to give it different meanings.

Putting material experience in terms of a "moment" allows standpoint theory to loosen its overfirm grasp without sacrificing its fundamental assertions about the concreteness, the "reality," of women's experiences. The idea of a materialist moment posits experience as having some prediscursive immediacy while simultaneously acknowledging the impossibility of ever capturing experience outside of discourse. It allows feminists to acknowledge the concreteness of experience within languages that have the denial of those experiences at their core while at the same time acknowledging that there is no way to share experience with others, or even to understand our own experiences, without those often hostile languages. It simultaneously recognizes that these experiences are in part functions of and created by language and that language can never, by its nature, contain the whole of such experiences. In the process, it also facilitates the transformation of language to reflect "nondiscursive" concrete experience more accurately, but it does so nonessentially because this transformation postulates neither timelessness, naturalness, nor universality. The fact that we treat it as a "moment" locates its specificity and temporality in the social processes of language without allowing language to supercede its "realness."

Perhaps most significant to standpoint feminism, a "materialist moment" provides feminists with a place to "stand." As Ferguson (1993) notes, "all feminist analyses . . . have to stand at least temporarily on some stable territory in order to bring other phenomena under scrutiny" (85). In order to critique discourse, in order to say "no" to the dominant picture of "reality," I have to stand somewhere else, in a different reality. Yet where can that reality lie if not in the always already patriarchal world? In a sense, I must be not "in" the world/discourse but, nevertheless, "of" it. It is this moment of possibility that a feminist standpoint struggles for. It is the dual positioning of experience as both discursive and nondiscursive that makes feminist critique and resistance possible. A "materialist moment" suggests that while experience exists in discourse, discourse is not the totality of experience: since experience may always be reinterpreted and redescribed, there must be something in experience that escapes, or is even prior to, language.[4] This "something" does not have an essential and timeless meaning; that is the point of viewing it as a "moment," something that gives way to and cannot maintain a sustained meaningful existence outside of discourse. And yet its independent existence, its "materiality," provides women with a "place to stand," even if only "momentarily," which allows us to see how we participate in our own social construction in ways that are both destructive (e.g., women's mothering supports and reinforces patriarchy) and productive (it also yields an ethics of care).

Perhaps even more importantly, it also points the way to more active theoretical and political construction (for instance, developing a new vision of politics *out of* care [Ruddick 1989]). At the same time, it allows us to be wary of this last step, to see that any construction can go off in different unforeseen directions with unintended consequences (e.g., white feminism's definition of a care ethics may perpetuate the erasure of women of color [see Collins 1990]). So it can help feminists be more self-critical and intellectually cautious even as we challenge, destabilize, and deconstruct patriarchy by creating new pictures of "reality."

These pictures involve, of course, new discourses. Treating materialism in terms of a *moment* reminds us of that and prevents the universalizing and essentializing potential of standpoint approaches. But it is important to recognize that these discourses come from material experiences. Naming this moment *materialist* emphasizes that new discourses do not just come out of other discourses but out of something more immediate and concrete. To say that experience is material, that it provides meaning that exists in part prior to discourse, does not mean the meaning is "natural," nor does it deny that it has to exist in discourse before political change can be effected. But it reminds us of a basic standpoint tenet that discourses are, at least in part, the result of "sensuous human activity, practice" (Hartsock 1983, 235, quoting Marx 1970, 121). Discourse and materiality are in close relationship, but they are, nevertheless, distinct. I do not simply "reinterpret" my experiences through a new discourse; experience also *enables* reinterpretation. Women's experiences are discursive, but they come, at least in part, from somewhere else, not "just" from discourse in an endless devolution. That such experience can be shared only *through* language is important to recognize. Indeed, it may be a crucial dimension of the standpoint notion of *shared* experience that we communicate about it through language, but discourse cannot exhaust the "reality" of experience.

CONCLUSION

Toward Postmodern Feminist Standpoints

I believe this recasting of Hartsock's formulation not only is a better representation of the implications of her argument, thus addressing some key postmodern objections, but it can also help bring together postmodern and standpoint feminism. In particular, by holding onto a nonessentializing notion of prediscurisive experience, the "materialist moment" strengthens the methodological power of multiple standpoints by helping feminists develop a more meaningful understanding of "difference." The danger of postmodern approaches to feminism is that by focusing on difference and particularity at the *exclusion* of commonality and sharing, the concept of difference becomes increasingly abstract, ill-defined, even unreal. At the same time, insistence on the discursivity of difference makes oppression difficult to identify, since power is "always and everywhere" in discourse, we are all constructors and constructed (Foucault 1990). Indeed, the possibility of language that can even articulate the character of particular differences must be called into question (Alcoff 1988). Without such articulation, however, relations of domination and oppression become invisible, or at least those who would name them are struck mute.

By working through "materialist moments," the notion of "difference" does not lose sight of oppression. As Bat-Ami Bar On (1993) observes, it is not enough for feminists to theorize difference, or even "marginality," for many differences are marginalized; rather we must understand how what is marginal is also central to patriarchal power relations. On my reading, standpoint feminism allows us to understand degrees of power and privilege that cohere to particular "differences" by holding onto the material reality of oppression. For instance, it allows the recognition that a Black feminist standpoint as a starting point for theory can reveal things about white women's experiences which a white feminist standpoint cannot reveal, precisely because of the privilege that adheres to being white (Harding 1991). A Black feminist standpoint is "less partial and perverse" because it sits at the fulcrum of intersecting vectors of oppression (Collins 1990).

At the same time, since many white women (of various other positionalities) do experience oppression and marginality, it makes no sense to ignore their experiences just because Black women are "more" oppressed or marginal. By that logic, we could simply find the most oppressed person and use her standpoint as the basis for a new true theory that tells the whole story. Even putting aside the incommensurability of certain oppressions–are Chicanas more oppressed in the United States than Blacks? Jews more than Muslims?–such a caricature of standpoint ignores the interdependence of different kinds of oppression and, hence, the need to articulate a variety of feminist standpoints (Hirschmann 1992).

Pursuing multiplicity within a feminist-standpoints' approach *and* locating such standpoints in materialist moments acknowledges a more complicated notion of oppression than the often simplistic Marxist-feminist formula where "men" oppress "women." At the same time, it prevents the slide into relativism so often typical of the postmodern emphasis on "difference" (McDowell 1992), for it provides a collective means of evaluating and discriminating between various claims to a standpoint. In order to count as a standpoint rather than a relativist "perspective" or an oppressive "ideology," it would have to establish itself as stemming from shared experiences of oppression. In order to count as "feminist," it would have to demonstrate that it led to the promotion of gender equality, a concept which must include racial, economic, and other kinds of equality since gendered subjects occupy multiple intersections of identity categories, without eliminating difference. It also must include an understanding of (some group of) *women's* lived experience. Thus contemporary white male claims of "reverse discrimination" caused by affirmative action, for instance, fail these criteria because they attend only to white men's experiences and interests.

The "materialist moment" also addresses a paradox that many theorists have noted: if a standpoint is based in experience, must one have that experience to have the standpoint? If so, then all that multiple standpoints would seem to do is multiply the various camps of epistemologically separated groups who, by definition, cannot communicate with one another. If not, however, then what is to stop those with privilege from defining the standpoints of less powerful people in ways that simply perpetuate, rather than challenge, existing power inequalities (Lennon 1995, 141-2)? The "materialist moment" takes a both/and approach to this problem: it allows for the adoption of standpoints not immediately out of one's own experience, but it requires that the discursive understanding come *from* the experience. As Uma Narayan (1989) argues:

> Our commitment to the contextual nature of knowledge does not require us to claim that those who do not inhabit these contexts can never have any knowledge of them. But this commitment does permit us to argue that it is *easier* and *more likely* for the oppressed to have critical insights into the conditions of their own oppression than it is for those who live outside those structures. Those who actually *live* the oppressions of class, race, or gender have faced the issues

that such oppressions generate in a variety of different situations. (264)

Such criteria allow the distinction between a standpoint and "ideology" which can be racist, misogynist, homophobic, classist, and so forth. A feminist-standpoints' approach acknowledges that men have insights to contribute to feminists, as do whites to African-Americans, heterosexuals to lesbians and gays. This is different from saying that "masculinism" has something to offer feminism, or "racism" has something to offer African-Americans, or "heterosexism" has something to offer lesbians and gays. The likelihood of masking ideology as standpoint is greater from the perspective of the more powerful in each of these pairs because such ideologies reinforce their preexisting claims to power. In keeping with Narayan's argument, the methodological advantage of standpoint epistemology for feminism lies in its notion that, at least at this point in history, women of various positionalities will be likely to have more to say to men of most positionalities about sexism. African-Americans would have more to say to whites about racism; and lesbians and homosexuals, more to say to heterosexuals about heterosexism because it considers the experiences of those oppressed by these ideologies and practices "less partial and perverse" than those of the more privileged position. The exchange of insights that follows from this is not exclusively from "the bottom up," but the burden of proof lies with the privileged, not the oppressed, to defend their vision of reality.

However, does all this make feminist standpoint a postmodern strategy? Or does it simply illustrate standpoint's (or perhaps my own) modernist blinders to the point that postmodernism is trying to make? It is a bit of both. We cannot get away from the fact that feminism is and must be in part a modernist discourse. Without the subject "woman," regardless of how we define it, feminism cannot exist; this subject, however, is at odds with postmodernism because it seems to freeze a notion of identity in time. *Standpoints'* feminism suggests that the definition of "who we are" will shift and change, in postmodern fashion, in response to different material conditions as well as to the fact that each individual occupies more than one experiential and identity location. This shifting within and between discourses and "materialist moments" does not mean that we cannot develop theories based on experience within particular and even contingent historical contexts. Indeed, we must. Hartsock's feminist standpoint theory allows us to occupy both theoretical positions at once and, thereby, provides a powerful and versatile strategy for addressing feminist theory's most contentious debates.

NOTES

1. The fact that this special volume is about "feminist standpoint theory" through the particular lens of Hartsock's work highlights the fact that Hartsock alone among the early standpoint theorists, such as Dorothy Smith and Sandra Harding, is a political scientist. Indeed, the fact that Hartsock's work has had such interdisciplinary impact from within political science is what led me to organize the 1994 APSA roundtable "The Feminist Standpoint: Ten Years Later," which in turn stimulated this *Women & Politics* special volume. The present paper is an expansion of my remarks on that panel. Thanks to panel participants, Sandra Harding, Susan Hekman, Sally Ruddick, Peregrine Schwartz-Shea, and most of all Nancy Hartsock, for whose personal and professional mentoring over the past fifteen years, I am truly grateful. Thanks also to the anonymous reviewers of *Women & Politics* as well as the guest editors of this volume for their helpful suggestions.

2. Similar errors are made by Susan Hekman (1990), who claims that Hartsock "has argued consistently that feminists must reject all epistemologies that are formulated by male theorists and adopt an epistemology that privileges the female standpoint" in direct contradiction to Hartsock's own statements; and by Jane Flax (1990), who, in apparent repudiation of her earlier reliance on standpoint theory (Flax 1983), claims that it presupposes "that people will act rationally on their 'interests' " again in direct contradiction to Hartsock's scathing critique of "market man's" psychology (Hartsock 1984, Chap. 7). Flax also maintains that the standpoint approach "assumes that the oppressed are not in some fundamental ways damaged by their social experience" (Flax 1990, 141), which ignores Hartsock's explicit acknowledgement of this paradoxical problem for standpoint theory (Hartsock 1984, 245).

3. If it lasted too long, of course, then the movement towards transformation would be lost; and once the moment is "frozen," it is no longer a moment but its own totalizing discourse. Hence, the temporal imagery suggested by the term "moment" indicates that it is part of a moving and shifting process; it cannot be static or stationary, for stasis lies outside of time.

4. I say "even" to note that "escaping" language is quite different from being "prior to" it. Even theorists like Butler (1993) suggest the possibility of that which "escapes" discourse, though she is extremely uncertain about how and even whether one could go about identifying it. Standpoint theory's materialist moment posits something more concrete than Butler would allow.

REFERENCES

Alcoff, Linda. 1988. "Cultural Feminism versus Poststructuralism: The Identity Crisis in Feminist Theory." *Signs: Journal of Women in Culture and Society* 13(3):405-36.

Alcoff, Linda and Elizabeth Potter, eds. 1993. *Feminist Epistemologies.* New York: Routledge.

Bar On, Bat-Ami. 1993. "Marginality and Epistemic Privilege." In *Feminist Epistemologies,* ed. Linda Alcoff and Elizabeth Potter. New York: Routledge.

Butler, Judith. 1990. *Gender Trouble: Feminism and the Subversion of Identity.* New York: Routledge.

Butler, Judith. 1993. *Bodies that Matter: On the Discursive Limits of "Sex."* New York: Routledge.

Collins, Patricia Hill. 1990. *Black Feminist Thought: Knowledge, Power, and the Politics of Empowerment.* New York: Unwin Hyman.

Cornell, Drucilla. 1993. *Transformations: Recollective Imagination and Sexual Difference.* New York: Routledge.

Ferguson, Kathy. 1993. *The Man Question: Visions of Subjectivity in Feminist Theory.* Berkeley: University of California Press.

Flax, Jane. 1983. "Political Philosophy and the Patriarchal Unconscious." In *Discovering Reality: Feminist Perspectives on Epistemology, Methodology, Metaphysics and Philosophy of Science,* ed. Sandra Harding and Merrill B. Hintikka. Boston: D. Reidel Publishing Co.

Flax, Jane. 1990. *Thinking Fragments: Feminism, Postmodernism, and Psychoanalysis.* Berkeley: University of California Press.

Foucault, Michel. 1990. *The History of Sexuality: Volume I, An Introduction.* New York: Vintage Books.

Fraser, Nancy and Linda Nicholson. 1990. "Social Criticism Without Philosophy: An Encounter Between Feminism and Postmodernism." *Feminism/Postmodernism,* ed. Linda Nicholson. New York: Routledge.

Grant, Judith. 1993. *Fundamental Feminism: Contesting the Core Concepts of Feminist Theory.* New York: Routledge.

Haraway, Donna J. 1991. *Simians, Cyborgs, and Women: The Reinvention of Nature.* New York: Routledge.

Harding, Sandra. 1986. *The Science Question in Feminism.* Ithaca: Cornell University Press.

Harding, Sandra. 1991. *Whose Science? Whose Knowledge? Thinking from Women's Lives.* Ithaca: Cornell University Press.

Hartsock, Nancy. 1981. "Political Change: Two Perspectives on Power." In *Building Feminist Theory: Essays from Quest, A Feminist Quarterly,* ed. Charlote Bunch. New York: Longman.

Hartsock, Nancy. 1983. "The Feminist Standpoint: Developing the Ground for a Specifically Feminist Historical Materialism." In *Discovering Reality: Feminist Perspectives on Epistemology, Methodology, Metaphysics and Philosophy of Science,* ed. Sandra Harding and Merrill B. Hintikka. Boston: D. Reidel Publishing Co.

Hartsock, Nancy. 1984. *Money, Sex, and Power: Toward a Feminist Historical Materialism.* Boston: Northeastern University Press.

Hartsock, Nancy. 1987. "Rethinking Modernism: Majority vs. Minority Theories." *Cultural Critique* 7:187-206.

Hartsock, Nancy. 1990. "Foucault on Power: A Theory for Women?" In *Feminism/ Postmodernism,* ed. Linda Nicholson. New York: Routledge.

Hawksworth, Mary. 1989. "Knowers, Knowing, Known: Feminist Theory and Claims of Truth." *Signs: Journal of Culture and Society* 14(3):533-57.

Hekman, Susan. 1990. *Gender and Knowledge.* Boston: Northeastern University Press.

Henwood, Karen L. and Nick F. Pidgeon. 1995. "Remarking the Link: Qualitive Research and Feminist Standpoint Theory." *Feminist & Psychology* 5(1):7-30.

Hennessy, Rosemary. 1993. *Materialist Feminism and the Politics of Discourse.* New York: Routledge.

Hirschmann, Nancy J. 1992. *Rethinking Obligation: A Feminist Method for Political Theory.* Ithaca: Cornell University Press.

Hirschmann, Nancy J. 1989. "Freedom, Recognition and Obligation: A Feminist Approach to Political Theory." *American Political Science Review* 83(4):1227-1244.

hooks, bell. 1984. *Feminist Theory: From Margin to Center.* Boston: South End Press.

Jaggar, Alison M. 1983. *Feminist Politics and Human Nature.* Totowa: Rowman and Allenheld.

Keller, Evelyn Fox. 1985. *Reflections on Gender and Science.* New Haven: Yale University Press.

Keohane, Robert. 1989. "International Relations Theory: Contributions of a Feminist Standpoint." *Millennium: Journal of International Studies* 18(2):2245-54.

Lennon, Kathleen. 1995. "Gender and Knowledge." *Journal of Gender Studies* 4(2):133-43.

Marx, Karl. 1970. "Theses on Feuerbach." In *The German Ideology,* ed. C.J. Arthur. New York: International Publishers.

McDowell, Linda. 1992. "Doing Gender: Feminism, Feminists, and Research Methods in Human Geography." *Transactions of the Institute of British Geographers* 17(4):399-416.

McLennon, Gregor 1995. "Feminism, Epistemology, and Postmodernism: Reflections on Current Ambivalence." *Sociology: The Journal of the British Sociological Association* 29:391-409.

Mohanty, Chandra. 1992. "Feminist Encounters: Locating the Politics of Experience." In *Destabilizing Theory,* ed. Michele Barrett and Ann Phillips. Oxford: Polity Press.

Narayan, Uma. 1989. "The Project of Feminist Epistemology: Perspectives from a Nonwestern Feminist." In *Gender/Body/ Knowledge: Feminist Reconstructions of Being and Knowing,* ed. Alison M. Jaggar and Susan R. Bordo. New Brunswick: Rutgers University Press.

Noddings, Nel. 1990. "Ethics from the Standpoint of Women." In *Theoretical Perspectives on Sexual Difference,* ed. Deborah L. Rhode. New Haven: Yale University Press.

Offen, Karen. 1990. "Feminism and Sexual Difference in Historical Perspective." In *Theoretical Perspectives on Sexual Difference,* ed. Deborah L. Rhode. New Haven: Yale University Press.

Ramazanoglu, Caroline. 1989. "Improving on Sociology: The Problems of Taking a Feminist Standpoint." *Sociology: The Journal of the British Sociological Association* 23(3):427-42.

Rixecker, Stefanie S. 1994. "Expanding the Discursive Context of Policy Design: A Matter of Feminist Standpoint Epistemology." *Policy Sciences* 27(2/3): 119-42.

Ruddick, Sarah. 1989. *Maternal Thinking: Toward a Politics of Peace.* New York: Basic Books.

Seller, Anne. 1994. "Should the Feminist Philosopher Stay at Home?" In *Knowing the Difference: Feminist Perspectives in Epistemology,* ed. Kathleen Lennon and Margaret Whitford. New York: Routledge.

Smith, Dorothy. 1990. *Texts, Facts, and Femininity: Exploring the Relations of Ruling.* New York: Routledge.

Spelman, Elizabeth V. 1988. *Inessential Woman: Problems of Exclusion in Feminist Thought.* Boston: Beacon Press.

Swigonski, Mary E. 1994. "The Logic of Feminist Standpoint Theory for Social Work Research." *Social Work: Journal of the National Association for Social Work Research* 39(4):387-93.

Sylvester, Christine. 1994. "Empathetic Cooperation: A Feminist Method for International Relations." *Millennium: Journal of International Studies* 23(2):315-34.

Weeks, Kathi. 1995. "Feminist Standpoint Theories and the Return of Labor." In *Marxism in the Postmodern Age: Confronting the New World Order,* ed. Antonio Callari, Stephen Cullenberg, and Carole Biewener. New York: Guilford Press.

Standpoint Theories
for the Next Century

Nancy C. M. Hartsock

My title may sound a bit overblown, but I do think that these articles as a group advance the discussion in many helpful ways, ways which complicate and extend it in directions appropriate to issues feminism faces at the end of the 1990s. They are of course more attuned to issues of difference than was my original essay—an important corrective. They all stress the ways in which feminist standpoint theories are concerned with epistemology and methodology rather than claims about what women in specific situations can be said to believe. And they all stress to different extent the fundamental political stakes involved in the construction of a standpoint and the claim of epistemological privilege these constructions generate.

As I have reflected on both these and other discussions of standpoint theories over the years, I have come to believe that it is this intertwining of issues of politics on the one hand with the more traditional philosophical questions concerning truth and knowledge on the other, along with their conflicting criteria for claims of epistemological validity which have been responsible for much of the controversy. That is, standpoint theories must be recognized as essentially contested in much the same way that I argued the concept of power was essentially contested: i.e., arguments about how

---

I would like to thank Sally J. Kenney for her work on conceiving and editing this special volume and for her patience in soliciting this comment. I would also like to thank Nancy Hirschmann for organizing the panel at the 1994 APSA meetings to consider standpoint theories. It is a great honor to have one's own work, and that of others with similar concerns, read with such care as the authors of the papers in this volume do.

[Haworth co-indexing entry note]: "Standpoint Theories for the Next Century." Hartsock, Nancy C. M. Co-published simultaneously in *Women & Politics* (The Haworth Press, Inc.) Vol. 18, No. 3, 1997, pp. 93-101; and: *Politics and Feminist Standpoint Theories* (ed: Sally J. Kenney and Helen Kinsella) The Haworth Press, Inc., 1997, pp. 93-101. Single or multiple copies of this article are available for a fee from The Haworth Document Delivery Service [1-800-342-9678, 9:00 a.m. - 5:00 p.m. (EST). E-mail address: getinfo@haworth.com].

to understand power rested on differing epistemologies. This may account for the existence of so many (conflicting) interpretations of the meaning of feminist standpoint theories. Two papers in this volume reflect such conflicting interpretations with Catherine Hundleby placing standpoint theories close to what Sandra Harding has identified as feminist empiricism, and Nancy Hirschmann stressing the postmodern tendencies latent in standpoint theories. And as readers of feminist theory will recognize, these do not exhaust the readings of standpoint theory.

Still, I prefer to see this proliferation of interpretation as an indication that standpoint theories represent a fertile terrain for feminist debates about power, politics, and epistemology. I believe, however, these papers address several important issues on which a great deal more work needs to be done. First, there is the question of the status of "experience" and its interpretation, most importantly the political consequences of treating experience in different ways. Second, particularly in the American (or perhaps Anglophone) context, much more needs to be learned about the constructions of group which must be thought of not as aggregations of individuals but as groups formed by their oppression and marginalization but sharing enough experiences to have the possibility of coming to understand their situation in ways that can empower their oppositional movements. Third, I believe there is a great deal of work to be done to elaborate the connections between politics, epistemology, and claims of epistemic privilege and to develop new understandings of engaged and accountable knowledge. These papers make some important contributions to these issues and help to set the agenda for development of standpoint theories which can contribute to the concerns of the next century.

At the same time they sometimes reflect formulations that I find very troubling. In particular, the status of the individual (and probably privileged and academic) knower sometimes takes too prominent a position. For example, Katherine Welton's use of Joan Scott's discussion of experience, where Scott argues that for those who claim experience is the foundation of knowledge it is the "vision of the individual subject" which becomes evidence (1992, 25). This erodes the importance of the epistemological collectivity in the production of standpoint analyses. Related to this problem is the tendency to descend into pluralism; e.g., Welton's suggestion that it is the interplay of standpoints which produces knowledge, with the implication that more knowledge is better than less, or Hundleby's suggestion that standpoints provide a greater volume of knowledge, which is then a good thing. The important questions are not quantitative and individual but collective and oppositional. But let me turn to a more direct consideration of each of the papers in turn.

Welton makes an excellent point when she argues that in my later work, rather than defining the content of a standpoint by labor, I leave the content of "concrete multiplicity," a different concept of standpoint, vague. I do so because I am less certain now about the importance of labor as a constitutive experience for different groups of people. Even though work is what most people do most of the time, I wonder if other activities can also be constitutive. In this I take some guidance from Fredric Jameson (1988) who suggests that in Eastern Europe fear and insecurity were central to the formation of Jewish identity as a people. At this point I think we need to collectively undertake a much more complex analysis of how women's labor is internationalized and integrated in the global economy—the specifics of women's work at the end of the millennium. And by this I want to point to the differential integration of women's paid and unpaid labor in the First and Third Worlds. I do not mean to suggest that the experience of the women who manufacture Nike shoes in Vietnam bears much similarity in the phenomenological specific to the lives of First World academic women. But I do want to suggest that we are linked in important ways which we need to understand more systematicly.

Welton also makes the point that I fail to specify how experience becomes mediated and transformed into a standpoint: I say no more than that knowledge grows in complex and contradictory way from experience. I can now add that I see this transformation as one that involves theoretical (but sometimes physical) migrations, learning to speak in a voice the dominant culture both suppresses and claims cannot exist and finally coming to see and name the ideology and social relations of the dominant culture as insane. That is what I meant by my discussion of abstract masculinity.

Too often, (though not by Welton) this process has been characterized as a discovery of the truth. And here, I think the influence of Marx's method on my work is elided. While this locution may represent the epistemology of the Enlightenment, in which the mind could discover truth while itself located nowhere, it is much more problematic as a description of Marx's method (unless, of course Marx is read as simply a modernist). For Marx, notions of a truth to be discovered by reason are extremely problematic in a world defined, structured, and even in a sense created by human activity, especially the activity of work. Moreover, given his argument that humans create the natural world as well as themselves, the place of reason seems quite subordinate. In addition, the role of reason is made more complex and peripheral by Marx's argument about the role of ideological reversals in capitalism, in which what seem to be relations between people are instead cast as relations between things.

Finally, rationalist ideas about the discovery of truth do not fit well with a methodology which redefines truth as "the reality and power of our ideas in action" and insists that the point is not to interpret the world but to change it. All this makes questionable any statement that Marx or Marxists are involved in an effort to discover truth, especially through reason. It rewrites Marx as an Enlightenment thinker and ignores his own profound anti-Enlightenment commitments. Hirschmann's paper is especially helpful on this issue as she suggests a way of re-reading standpoint theories which points toward the possibility of re-readng Marx as a postmodernist thinker. This could lead to a re-discovery of the utility of Marxist analysis for understanding the present world where the triumph of commodification has advanced to new heights.

But to return more explicitly to the process by which consciousness is changed or experience reinterpreted in standpoint terms, I think it is worth remembering that the vision of the ruling groups structures the material relations in which all parties are forced to participate and, therefore, cannot be dismissed as simply false. (Given this formulation, I would like to underline once again the extent to which claims that interpretation is involved in an effort to discover truth are problematic.) Truth is, to a large extent, what the dominant groups can make true; history is always written by the winners. Thus the understanding available to the oppressed must be struggled for and represents an achievement that requires both systematic analysis and the education which grows from political struggle to change those relations. This point is also the key to the reason I chose the term "feminist" standpoint. Rather than the standpoint of women.

The process of adopting a standpoint, or in other terms developing an oppositional consciousness, is described by Gloria Anzaldua in a quotation by Catherine O'Leary. "The process is inner . . . the struggle has always been inner and is played out in outer terrains" (1987, 87). One's location in the social structure does not change, but the understanding of its meaning shifts dramatically. In these terms the work of Michelle Cliff is particularly instructive. She describes the difficulty she had, a light-skinned, Jamaican woman with a PhD concerning the Italian Renaissance, in coming to approach herself as a subject or, in my terms, adopting a standpoint. She states, in "Notes on Speechlessness" that she had internalized the "message of anglocentrism, of white supremacy" (1985, 13). She notes that she began, through participation in the feminist movement, to retrace the African part of herself and to reclaim it. She is clear about the difficulty of the project. In an earlier book, she says that she wrote as someone who was unable to "recapture the native language of Jamaica" and so relied on English but still wrote from a feminist consciousness, a consciousness of colonialism, and a knowledge of self-hatred (1985, 16). As she began to write in a way that put her own identity and experience at the center, she notes that her writing style became a kind of shorthand. "Write quickly before someone catches you. Before you catch yourself" (1985, 16). Her writing is informed by and structured by her rage and marks very clearly the struggle, both political and personal, involved in taking up a position from which the dominant order becomes visible with all its distortions.

Michelle Cliff's struggles are illustrative as well to the final charge leveled against my essay: that I am describing a "women's perspective" constituted by oppression and unaware of its complicity in the oppression of others. As is evident from my discussion of the achieved character of a standpoint, it is constituted by more than oppression. Fredric Jameson (1988, 67) has probably put it most clearly when he states that the experience of negative constraint and violence, the commodification of labor power dialectically produces the positive content of its experience as the self consciousness of the commodity. Once again, Michelle Cliff's work is instructive. She looks back, to try to locate what happened: "When did *we* (the light-skinned, middle-class Jamaicans) take over for *them* as oppressors?" (1985, 67). Cliff is clearly conscious about her complicity with imperialism and racism. It is a central aspect of her ability to locate herself in a critical context.

In addition, Cliff writes of the "insanity" and "unreality" of the "normal." She writes of light-skinned, middle-class Jamaicans that "we were colorists and we aspired to oppressor status. . . . We were convinced of white supremacy. If we failed, our dark part had taken over: an inherited imbalance in which the doom of the creole was sealed." She steps back to look at what she has written and states that this "may sound fabulous, or even mythic. It is. It is insane" (1988, 78).

Moreover, I see Cliff and Anzaldua and others as developing a kind of privileged knowledge which takes nothing of the dominant culture as self-evidently true. The privilege is earned by means of the struggle to overcome what the dominant culture tells us about the world and ourselves, the struggle to construct and live in a political community and to build with it an accountable epistemological community.

I found myself confused by Catherine Hundleby's paper, since it reads like two different papers. The first part is marked by troubling suggestions that standpoints simply provide a greater volume of knowledge. But as I noted above this kind of quantitative analysis is not what standpoint theories are about. Moreover, the "rigorous methods of science" she mentions are themselves implicated in power relations which standpoint theorists oppose and seek to transform. In addition, the author seems to make some unnecessary mistakes when she conflates empiricism with empirical work and suggests that Harding's concept of "strong objectivity" is an empiricist notion. I am also troubled by her seeming acceptance of the objection to my arguing that women are closer to nature as implying "their lesser competence at culture." From a Marxist perspective we are both human and natural, and interaction with nature to create subsistence is what makes us human. Thus, nature itself is a form of human work, since we duplicate ourselves actively and come to contemplate the selves we have created in a world of our own making (1964,112). Moreover Haraway has argued strongly that the nature/culture split must be refused. The natural sciences themselves must be seen as culturally constructed and as cultural artifacts. As she puts it, "we both learn about and create nature and ourselves." Science is culture as she puts it, and one might say as well that nature is culture (Haraway 1991, 230). Finally, I do not see it as a statement about the virtues of feminist empiricism to note that its "epistemological Pedigree" is more acceptable than Marxism, and to let stand Campbell's argument that feminist empiricism can have a more successful theoretical career in part because it is less confrontational.

But then the paper seems to change direction and recognizes that developing a standpoint is something which is created and must be self consciously located in terms of group memberships. Most succinctly and more clearly than I have been able to say it, she states "A standpoint is a political construction." In addition, she makes the very important but all too often missed point (in our individualist culture) that a standpoint does not privilege the position of the individual knower. Indeed, it is the individual knower's lack of separate and isolated individuality which allows for the transformation of individual experiences into collective knowledge usable for political contestation. I think in her use of Collins to stress the importance of group membership Hundleby explicitly recognizes the political stakes in standpoint theory. Her conclusion is worthy of Marx's own understanding of history; she suggests that standpoint theories operate to rush toward their "own demise by addressing the epistemic significance of oppression." I had not recognized the importance of standpoint theories themselves as historical and changing artifacts, although that is, I think, one of the central lessons of this set of essays. And here I think she once again very succinctly holds together in tension the two aspects of standpoint theory which many have split apart. It is about epistemology, better knowledge, but that better knowledge is inseparable from its political motivation and force. She has located one of the central difficulties for academic treatments of standpoint theories and put together a formulation which grasps the core of the problem.

O'Leary begins her paper with an important point that the epistemological implications of race, class, sex, sexuality, and nation have not been broadly recognized in feminist theory. She goes on to say that only sociological attention has been paid. And she is right–certainly about my work. My work in the 1983 essay ran into difficulties, ironically by following Marx too closely. Thus, despite the fact that he recognized that the situation of women was less than satisfactory, that bourgeois marriage was a form of prostitution, that widows were part of the lowest layer of the reserve army of the unemployed, he lost track of women's labor in reproducing the working class. And so at the heart of his theory–the theory of how surplus value is produced and extracted–women are not present. Thus he was, if I understand O'Leary's point correctly, taking only a sociological view of the situation of women without recognizing the epistemological potentials that he did recognize for male workers. By relying too closely on Marx's procedure in reducing the world to a two class, two man model, I ended up with the same problem for which I criticized him in *Money, Sex, and Power*: recognizing important axes of domination but unable to understand their epistemological significance. Thus, just as Marx subsumed women under the category "man," I ended up subsuming the "marked" categories of feminists under the unmarked and, therefore, white feminist and lesbian under the category of straight. So despite my recognition of their situations, my treatment was in fact only sociological. This is an important criticism that should be more widely recognized and guarded against in feminist theory. The statement by hooks at the beginning of her paper as well as the work by Collins, which do attend to the epistemological significance of race, can provide some methodological advice for others on how to recognize and enhance the features of the social existence of other groups that can provide possibilities for alternative epistemological and political standpoints.

I am disappointed, however, that O'Leary conflates my work and that of Jaggar, since although she recognizes the significance of my use of the term "feminist standpoint," she still titles the section on Jaggar's and my work "Women's Standpoint Theory." Her discussion has several flaws from my perspective: she seems to think that there can be such a thing as a "detached standpoint," e.g., of liberal theory, and even characterizes John Rawls' original position behind the veil of ignorance as a standpoint. But a standpoint is not a simply a perspective and cannot escape political as well as epistemological issues. As Katie King (1994, 62) puts it in her excellent discussion of my project and Jaggars' (and using the same statement by bell hooks as appears at the beginning of O'Leary's essay), a standpoint has "an inverse relation to the possession of privilege." She goes on to state that a standpoint can only be constructed by those in a "marked" rather than unmarked category (1994, 62). I think she is right that Jaggar's discussion of women's standpoint comes later in the debates about feminist theory. She notes that my essay had circulated in manuscript for several years before it was published and that I was responding to some of the issues characteristic of 1980 more than was Jaggar. So in a sense we were operating in two different moments of feminist time, one before and the other after the very important interventions by women of color at the 1981 NWSA.

O'Leary's use of Collins and hooks points to the difference epistemological treatments of subjectivity can make. In addition, it is central to both their work that they are members of marked groups, unlikely to mistake themselves for the unmarked individual subject, and sharing the experiences of being marked, made into groups, by the dominant culture.

Finally, I think O'Leary's concept of coalition as a "second" moment of standpoint theories is a valuable formulation of what many feminists—including, of course, those she cites–have been discussing. It is also important that the discussion concludes not with concerns about knowledge and truth but about political action. The linking of epistemological concerns with political action lies at the heart of feminist standpoints.

Nancy Hirschmann very eloquently and subtly pulls out my unstated and (probably in many cases) unknown assumptions. She significantly expands and extends the possibilities in standpoint theories and makes standpoint theory much more friendly to postmodern concerns with issues of difference. I think her reading of my essay and others searches out and develops possibilities of recognizing that standpoint theories rely on social construction theories of human subjectivity. Moreover, her strong emphasis on the argument that standpoint theories are methodological tools which can be used to transform understanding of experience makes clearer, than do any other authors I can think of, the basis for "translating" or rather, perhaps, recognizing that the construction of a political community can (and perhaps must) be at the same time the construction of an epistemological community.

But somehow the concept of experience as it "really" or "immediately" is is troubling. Experience, identity, and knowledge are all contested terms in discussions of standpoint theories. The point of the methodological guidance that standpoint theories try to give is that understanding experience is not at all simple; and moreover, it cannot be understood simply by an individual acting alone (a type of private language). Still, I see her insistence on standpoint theories as epistemological as an important correction to readings of standpoint theories as describing women's viewpoints. The truly difficult task is to understand both how language affects the interpretation of experience, and how language at the same time does not completely structure our experience. But the problem is how to name and, most importantly, redescribe the experience and, in so doing, change the nature of that experience.

In the context of O'Leary's designation of coalition as the second moment of standpoint theories, Hirschmann's discussion of the materialist moment gains more significance. Perhaps the materialist moment is the first moment with coalition the second. I think the concept of moment is a very useful one, not so much referring to a clock but to a series of debates which are located in and define a particular political conjunction. In terms of thinking about the development of standpoint theories more adequate to our current situation, perhaps the concept of "moment" is one of the most important to emerge from these essays. The tasks for each moment differ, depending on particular political conjunctions. Following Bernice Reagon, there are moments when political/epistemological communities must be forged but other moments when the tasks are different. The two papers taken together suggest that we should perhaps begin to think about what a third moment will look like.

I think that one of the issues all the papers raise is the idea that feminist standpoint arguments about methodology could be helped a great deal by explicit attention to those epistemological issues. But they all work to complicate and revise standpoint theories to be more responsive to the issues we face at the end of the 1990s. As such, I see this volume as a valuable contribution to the development of feminist theory.

REFERENCES

Anzaldua, Gloria. 1987. *Borderlands/La Frontera: The New Mesiza.* San Francisco: Spinsters/Aunt Lute.
Cliff, Michelle. 1985. *The Land of Look Behind.* Ithaca: Firebrand Books.
Cliff, Michelle. 1988. "Speaking from Silence." In *Graywolf Annual Five: Multicultural Literacy,* ed. Rick Simonson and Scott Walker. St. Paul: Graywolf Press.
Haraway, Donna. 1991. *Simians, Cyborgs, and Women.* New York: Routledge.
Jameson, Fredric. 1988. "History and Class Consciousness as an 'Unfinished Product.'" *Rethinking Marxism* 1(1):49-72.
King, Katie. 1994. *Theory in Its Feminist Travels.* Bloomington: Indiana University Press.
Marx, Karl. 1964. *Econcomic and Philosophic Manuscripts of 1844* (Dirk Struik, ed.). New York: International Press.
Scott, Joan W. 1992. "Experience." In *Feminists Theorize The Political,* ed. Judith Butler and Joan W. Scott. New York: Routledge.

About the Contributors

NANCY C. M. HARTSOCK teaches political science, feminist theory, and women's studies at the University of Washington. She is the author of *Money, Sex, and Power: Toward a Feminist Historical Materialism* and is co-editor of *Building Feminist Theory: Essays from Quest* and *Women's Poverty.*

NANCY J. HIRSCHMANN is Associate Professor of Government at Cornell University. She is the author of *Rethinking Obligation: A Feminist Method for Political Theory* (1992, Cornell University Press) and co-editor with Christine Di Stefano of *Revisioning the Political: Feminist Reconstructions of Traditional Concepts in Western Political Theory* (1996, Westview Press). She is currently writing a book on a feminist approach to freedom.

CATHERINE HUNDLEBY is a PhD candidate studying epistemology in the Department of Philosophy at the University of Western Ontario, Canada.

SALLY J. KENNEY is Associate Professor of Public Policy at the Humphrey Institute of Public Affairs at the University of Minnesota and the co-director of the Center on Women and Public Policy. She is the author of *For Whose Protection? Reproductive Hazards and Exclusionary Policies in the United States and Britain* (University of Michigan Press, 1992). She is currently doing research on the European Court of Justice.

HELEN KINSELLA is a PhD candidate in political science at the University of Minnesota. She has an MA in public affairs from the Humphrey Institute and a graduate minor in feminist studies. Her research focuses on international networks on violence against women, Latin American politics, and feminist political theory.

CATHERINE O'LEARY is a PhD candidate in the Department of Political Science at the New School for Social Research. Her dissertation is a study of culture as a site of political inequality in the case of education reform politics in New York and Chicago. Her research interests include feminist theory, critical race theory, and American political development. She is currently a Visiting Predoctoral Fellow at the Institute for Policy Research at Northwestern University.

KATHERINE WELTON is a PhD candidate in the Department of Government at the University of Queensland, Australia. She is currently completing a doctorate on the concept of objectivity in feminist theories of knowledge.

Index

Academics, feminist, 14-15
Accountability,
        33,46,49,50-51,67,70n.
Affirmative action, as reverse
        discrimination, 87
African-American feminism, 2,3
African-American feminists
    consciousness of, 62
    standpoint of, 48,78,86
African-American women
    collective identity of,
        37,61-62,63,64-65
    experience of, 37,62,63-64
    as marginalized group, 86
    oppression of, 35,37,62
Afro-centrism, epistemological, 62
Alarcón, Norma
    criticism of standpoint theory by,
        50,58,59-61
    "Theoretical Subject(s) of *This
        Bridge Called My Back* and
        Anglo-American
        Feminism," 59
American Political Science
        Association, 1
Anglo-centrism, of white supremacy,
        96
Anzaldúa, Gloria, 50,96,97
Arendt, Hannah, 12
Autonomy, 59,62

Betzner, Ann, 4
Biological basis
    of the division of labor, 81
    of standpoint theory, 75
Biological sciences, effect of
        standpoint theory on, 73

Black power movement, 64
Bourgeois women
    class consciousness of, 54
    feminism of, 59

Capitalism, 9,75,95
Casale, Oriane, 4
Child-rearing, 53
Chomsky, Carol, 4
Class
    epistemological significance of,
        48,99
    Marxist analysis of, 55
    relationship to gendered aspects
        of labor, 78
Class consciousness, 54
Class exploitation, 49
Classism, 33
Cliff, Michelle, 96-97
Coalition, 50-51,65-68,100,101
"Coalition Politics: Turning the
        Century" (Reagon), 65-66
Collins, Patricia Hill, 1,3,16,34-35,
        37,50,61-63,99,100
    "The Social Construction of
        Black Feminist Thought,"
        62
Colonialism, 49,54,96-97
Commodification, 96,97
Communitarian theory, 12
Communities/groups, 37,38
    dominant
        experience and perspective of,
        11
        power within, 60

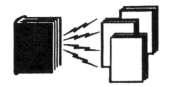

Haworth
DOCUMENT DELIVERY
SERVICE

This valuable service provides a single-article order form for any article from a Haworth journal.

- *Time Saving:* No running around from library to library to find a specific article.
- *Cost Effective:* All costs are kept down to a minimum.
- *Fast Delivery:* Choose from several options, including same-day FAX.
- *No Copyright Hassles:* You will be supplied by the original publisher.
- *Easy Payment:* Choose from several easy payment methods.

Open Accounts Welcome for . . .
- Library Interlibrary Loan Departments
- Library Network/Consortia Wishing to Provide Single-Article Services
- Indexing/Abstracting Services with Single Article Provision Services
- Document Provision Brokers and Freelance Information Service Providers

MAIL or *FAX* THIS ENTIRE ORDER FORM TO:

Haworth Document Delivery Service
The Haworth Press, Inc.
10 Alice Street
Binghamton, NY 13904-1580

or FAX: 1-800-895-0582
or CALL: 1-800-342-9678
9am-5pm EST

PLEASE SEND ME PHOTOCOPIES OF THE FOLLOWING SINGLE ARTICLES:
1) Journal Title: _____
　　Vol/Issue/Year:_____Starting & Ending Pages:_____
　　Article Title:_____
_____

2) Journal Title: _____
　　Vol/Issue/Year:_____Starting & Ending Pages:_____
　　Article Title:_____
_____

3) Journal Title: _____
　　Vol/Issue/Year:_____Starting & Ending Pages:_____
　　Article Title:_____
_____

4) Journal Title: _____
　　Vol/Issue/Year:_____Starting & Ending Pages:_____
　　Article Title:_____
_____

(See other side for Costs and Payment Information)

COSTS: Please figure your cost to order quality copies of an article.

1. Set-up charge per article: $8.00
   ($8.00 × number of separate articles)   _____

2. Photocopying charge for each article:

   1-10 pages: $1.00   _____

   11-19 pages: $3.00   _____

   20-29 pages: $5.00   _____

   30+ pages: $2.00/10 pages   _____

3. Flexicover (optional): $2.00/article   _____

4. Postage & Handling: US: $1.00 for the first article/

   $.50 each additional article   _____

   Federal Express: $25.00   _____

   Outside US: $2.00 for first article/
   $.50 each additional article _____

5. Same-day FAX service: $.35 per page   _____

GRAND TOTAL: _____

METHOD OF PAYMENT: (please check one)

❑ Check enclosed   ❑ Please ship and bill. PO # _____
(sorry we can ship and bill to bookstores only! All others must pre-pay)

❑ Charge to my credit card: ❑ Visa; ❑ MasterCard; ❑ Discover;
❑ American Express;

Account Number:_____ Expiration date:_____

Signature: **✗**_____

Name: _____ Institution: _____

Address: _____

_____

City: _____ State:_____ Zip:_____

Phone Number: _____ FAX Number: _____

MAIL or *FAX* THIS ENTIRE ORDER FORM TO:

Haworth Document Delivery Service	**or FAX:** 1-800-895-0582
The Haworth Press, Inc.	**or CALL:** 1-800-342-9678
10 Alice Street	9am-5pm EST)
Binghamton, NY 13904-1580	